Eloquence

2015 Poetry Collection

Eloquence represents our student authors as accurately as possible.
Every effort has been made to print each poem
as it was submitted with minimal editing
of spelling, grammar, and punctuation.
All submissions have been formatted to this compilation.

Published by
The America Library of Poetry
P.O. Box 978
Houlton, ME 04730
Website: www.libraryofpoetry.com
Email: generalinquiries@libraryofpoetry.com

Printed in the United States of America.

THE AMERICA
LIBRARY OF POETRY

ISBN: 978-0-9966841-0-1

Contents

In Memory Of 4
Foreword 5
About the Editor's Choice Award 6
Spirit of Education Award 7

Poetry by Division

Division I
Grades 3-5 9

Division II
Grades 6-7 61

Division III
Grades 8-9 141

Division IV
Grades 10-12 197

Index of Authors 218

Ordering Eloquence 223

Eloquence

In memory of two of our student authors
Jay'Von Quarles and Tianna Booqua

Weightlifting
by Jay'Von Quarles
(November 7, 1997 – August 13, 2015)

Benching and cleaning
Going to a competition and winning
I'm stronger than average
When I start lifting, I become savage
I'm a beast in the weight room
When I drop heavy weight it makes a big BOOM
Weightlifting is my passion
When I'm lifting, shorts and a ripped shirt is my fashion

Destroyed
by Tianna Booqua
(November 17, 2000 – September 15, 2015)

This is what leads many to cut.
Many would like the help, but don't have the guts to ask.
They think their few words don't matter,
In reality those few words could save some lives.
Every day their hate builds, weighing them down.
In place of their usual smile is a frown.
Being singled out for something they did wrong.
Most of the time it's hard for them to stay strong.
They begin to think the only way out is death.
Think that is the only way they can get a rest.
Maybe we could stand up to that one bully at school,
Tell them what they're doing is cruel.
Yes, maybe we could stand up for our fellow peers,
Maybe we could see them live an extra couple of years.
You never realize what you say
'Cause their smiles are just like Band-Aids,
But in reality what you say hurts more the next day.
You may think it's funny.
Until someone is six feet under.

Foreword

There are two kinds of writers in the world.
There are those who write from experience,
and those who write from imagination.
The experienced, offer words that are a reflection of their lives.
The triumphs they have enjoyed, the heartaches they have endured;
all the things that have made them who they are,
they graciously share with us, as a way of sharing themselves,
and in doing so, give us, as readers, someone to whom we may relate,
as well as fresh new perspectives
on what may be our common circumstances in life.
From the imaginative,
come all the wonderful things we have yet to experience;
from sights unseen, to sounds unheard.
They encourage us to explore the limitless possibilities
of our dreams and fantasies,
and aid us in escaping, if only temporarily,
the confines of reality and the rules of society.
To each, we owe a debt of gratitude;
and rightfully so, as each provides a service of equal importance.
Yet, without the other, neither can be truly beneficial.
For instance, one may succeed in accumulating a lifetime of experience,
only to consider it all to have been predictable and unfulfilling,
if denied the chance to chase a dream or two along the way.
Just as those whose imaginations run away with them never to return,
may find that without solid footing in the real world,
life in fantasyland is empty.
As you now embark, dear reader,
upon your journey through these words to remember,
you are about to be treated to both heartfelt tales of experience,
and captivating adventures of imagination.
It is our pleasure to present them for your enjoyment.
To our many authors,
who so proudly represent the two kinds of writers in the world,
we dedicate this book, and offer our sincere thanks;
for now, possibly more than ever,
the world needs you both.

Paul Wilson Charles
Editor

Editor's Choice Award

The Editor's Choice Award is presented
to an author who demonstrates not only
the solid fundamentals of creative writing,
but also the ability to elicit an emotional response
or provide a thought provoking body of work
in a manner which is both clear and concise.

You will find "Industria and Acedia"
by Madison Seabrook on page 217 of Eloquence

2015
Spirit of Education
For Outstanding Participation

Western Pines
Middle School

West Palm Beach
Florida

Presented to participating students and faculty
in recognition of your commitment
to literary excellence.

Division I

Grades
3-5

I Used To Have You
by Michaela Joniec

I used to have life, but now I have nothing.
I used to have friends, but now I let them go.
I used to have family, but now I'm alone.
I wonder how much they've grown.
I used to be an angel, but now I'm a devil.
I used to be on top, but now I'm below.
I used to be tough, but now I'm weak.
I used to be bold, but now I'm bleak.
I'm so weak.

Dreams
by Amos Klempel

Dreams, dreams the things at night.
The things that might go bump in the night.
They may be good, they may be bad.
The older you get, the less you have.
So savor those dreams.
The ones that you remember.
Write them down.
Make a song.
Just have some fun.
Dreams are good, dreams are bad.
But savor them anyway.

I'm Not Lonely, I Have God
by Nevaeh Everett

I am not lonely, I have God.
He is watching me everywhere I go.
I know He's there 'cause I feel Him so.
When I do something wrong He forgives my sin
Even when it first began.
At church we pray for the people that did us wrong.
We forgive them as we go along.
If you're praying to a different God it's okay.
We accept the way you are.
God will not be outdone.

Video Joe
by Nicholas Remacle

Video Joe is a jolly old lad,
he likes to make videos,
he is totally rad,
he uses his recorder,
his video taper
to make awesome videos,
for his awesome fans.

Music
by Mya Madden

Beautiful, sweet sounds
echoing through the room,
while little girls dance,
to the very sweet tune
Music tells a story
that couldn't otherwise be told
About anything and everything perhaps, the whole world
Children dancing, singing, humming and laughing
As the music plays through the room
Children listen to the music
Adults listen to the music,
And everybody listens to the music

School
by Jaleigh Richmond

Come on, come on, school is in.
Take out a book, read it
ok all done, wasn't that fun.
Ya ya hooray for us.
Look around at all your friends.
Look at all those grins.
Look at them oh so happy, happy as can be.
I do love my friends dearly.
We may fight some and not some
but we will always come as happy as can be,
and till on I will always be happy.
Goodbye!
Goodbye!

Feelings
by Tony Perez

What do you see?
And how do you feel when you see it
When I see a commercial for abandoned dogs
It makes me feel sad
When I see fireworks, they make me feel
Excited or happy
When I see the sunset
It gives me mixed emotions
What do you see?
And how do you feel when you see it

Friendship Is Forever
by Valkyrie Jade Tirtakusuma

Some people could be your friend
Friends are valuable
They're a nice thing to have
It's better not to have enemies
Enemies are mean and worthless
Enemies are bad things to have
Friendship has to be built
Friendship means you always talk nice
Friendship doesn't have popularity
Friendship accepts who you are
Because friendship is forever

You Are My Light
by Allison Gardner

You are a light in my path, you shine like a star and you are super bright.
You are like my kite that never falls and is always soaring high.
You never fight me, you never bite me.
You always write me letters when I'm not happy.
You give me all your might and courage when I get scared.
You keep me nice and warm at night, you comfort me when I get frightened.
You help me when I get a dark feeling and help me feel better.
You also take me to the most outstanding sites,
You are my light!

My Blanket
by Alaina Hadley

My blanket is warm
For the winter
I love my blanket
It's nice and cuddly
Sweet and warm
My blanket, my blanket
I love my blanket

Bubble Gum
by Nicole Hopkins

Yum, yum, bubble gum
chew it up, chew it down,
you can chew it out of town.
Chew it once, chew it twice,
Bubble gum is very nice.
Chew it here, chew it there,
you can chew it anywhere
Yum, yum, bubblc gum.

Brotherly Love
by Sean C. Harrington

As I hear my alarm yelling,
"Get up, gct up!"
I open my eyes and see my window fogging up
I get out of bed with surprise
My brother says, "Goodbye."
Then I realize, "I'm late for school."
I ran out of my house
As quick as a mouse
I wanted to punish him for not waking me
But I couldn't hurt him
He got cuter and cuter
I know we love each other so much
He and I
Are a brother bunch!

A Message To Not Take Drugs
by Thomas Cerruti

When I was a young man
I took a stand
I decided to say no
Now my body continues to grow.

Guardian Angel
by Elle Wagner Uhling

As time goes by I wonder, do you still remember me
do I still remember you
No words can explain the way I'm missing you
this emptiness inside,
Then one night there you were in my dream
standing there perfectly
it all comes back to me
your touch, your voice, your smile, your laughter
Then I knew, from that moment, I will never forget you again
I love you, Mom

In My Imagination
by Allison Remacle

In my imagination I am a fairy,
Flitting around and hiding from humans
In my imagination I am a superhero,
Saving the town from all evil
In my imagination I am a mermaid,
Singing a sweet tune to my little pet fish
In my imagination I am a dragon,
Flying above, flapping my great big wings
In my imagination I am a unicorn,
Prancing around finding rainbows to chase
In my imagination I am a princess,
Waiting for my prince in a tower
In my imagination I am a giant,
Taller than tall could ever be
In my imagination I am a very nice monster,
Giving very furry hugs to little ones
In my imagination I can be everything
Be anything, see anything, and be me!

Put the Dreams In My Head
by Ryan Wenclewicz

The dream that seems to come the most
Is the one that is a ton of fun, when I'm the richest one.
Now I am the leader of dreamers and I help everyone that yelps for help.
Ever since I saw John the angel on the cloud, I have been yelping for help
In my bed or anywhere I go. Sally helps me when I yelp for help or other people
That yelp for help.

The War
by Jeffrey Trimble

Cold, scared, frustrated, dark,
The sound of swords hitting each other.
I hear people yelling, "Man down!" repeatedly,
People fighting for their lives.
It went on like this for five days,
Then we finally hear the enemy yell,
"We surrender"

Baking and Making
by Hailey Whitlock

I love to bake,
For heaven's sake.
Mixing the batter at low speed,
Is fun for you and me.
The smell of things baking is delish,
Just like a wish.
I make frosting from scratch,
That no other baker can match.
It's piping hot and must cool,
Before tomorrow, when I take it to school.
I pack it so neat,
So it looks like a treat.
My friends see me and smile,
Even mean mug Kyle.
My heart pounds,
As they did in and do not make a sound.
With eyes wide open and mouths full, they make a big deal,
And true happiness I feel.
BAKERS RULE!

Spring
by Kevin Garcia

Spring has slowly come.
Flowers peek through the soil.
Sunshine fills the air.

You and Me
by Macie Dirickson

We can roam free, you see
you and me
Soar the skies until we die
run or walk
We don't have to talk
as long as we're hand in hand
We can be together forever
We can stay or
we can play
We can snooze
you can choose
I really don't mind
as long as you're mine

Life Line
by Matthew Black

The sea is the skyline,
The skyline's the sea,
The world is my lifetime,
My lifetime is me.
The heartbeat of lions,
The heartbeat of mice,
They bring me the warmth,
Of the fires of ice.
Nobody looks,
Nobody stares,
We all know the power,
Of heart's tender care.
The sun gives us fire,
Fire makes heat,
No one is perfect,
Everyone's we.

The Wand
by Corey Beougher

Whoosh, bang, fizzle, sssssss
The wand was waved again
Whoosh, bang, fizzle, sssssss

Dreams
by Sera Durtschi

When I dream
I dream of things
Like candy canes and magical things
That run around my mind
And when I dream
You'll find me sleeping
And if you don't
I might be daydreaming.
Some dreams can be scary
Like falling off a cliff
Or dying
But I'm always going to be dreaming
Day and night
Forever and always

Christmas Mouse
by Aaron Bagley

Christmas bells ring
So I start to sing
I go around my house
And sing about a mouse
I thought I heard a squeak
So I peek
And see a mouse with pink
The mouse starts to squeak
I listened to the tune
And then sing about a spoon
I wish Christmas could stay
But I can play
With the mouse I met that day

Reading
by Gage Berry

I like reading books.
A book is imagination on a page.
You can read about crooks
You can read about mages.
You can always read about more
Reading is no waste of time.
Just don't read about war
Some books even rhyme.
You can learn about farms
Reading even helps you learn.
Some books have harm
When you read just don't burn.

Wild Mustangs In the Wind
by Payton Mayes

Running free in the wind chased by a
Country rider, yes it is true,
Just don't doubt it
Just like you have to try it,
The eagle soars across the land,
As you are being chased by a
Country rider.
By the time you see they captured you
Herd you look back,
As you're being captured you are being
Taken to a dark and scary place,
you are being loaded into a trailer,
As your herd is having a fright in their eyes
The newborn colt,
Is being scared and frightened,
You do not know what to do,
But you sense your feelings
Are being thrown away by feeling scared.

Lego, Lego, Lego
by Korby Lindsey

Lego, Lego, Lego, how come they're so fun
Everybody likes them because they are so fun.
Even if you don't, you won't dislike them for long
Because they are so fun.
You can build your imagination.
When you're having fun.

Summer
by Ciara Fall

Kids are waiting for the bell to ring,
Waiting to race through the doors,
Ready to jump out of their seats,
As the teachers make the last announcements
the children hop up,
The bell finally rang,
Students race to the door,
The time has come,
Summer has begun.

Susi Sensi
by Logan Fredericksen

Susi Sensi on the day of Pompeii
Went to play then ate some hay
At the Bay of Pompeii
It was quite a day.
So on that bad day of Pompeii
Susi Sensi stayed in Hotel Lousay
And said I'm Mrs. Sensi, Lady of Pompeii
And I wish you all a very good day.
Just then she saw a blue jay
That said, "Run run the fires of Pompeii"
So she got her bale and said, "What a day."

Doug the Slug
by Trecon Talbot

My name is Doug
I am a slug
I'm really slow
But that's how I roll.
I eat ice cream.
I don't like to dream.
I like to play sports,
I like to build forts
I have lots of friends
And also trends.
One of them is Jake,
He is a rake,
Another is a boa
Constrictor,
Take a picture.
James is the best,
He likes to rest,
It's time to go,
See ya, Yo.

Cheerleading
by Tiernee Johnson

I am a cheerleader,
I have always loved cheerleading
I have been doing it since I was 4
It has been my dream to go to Worlds,
This year I am going to Summit,
Summit is like a mini Worlds,
It is a very big deal
One thing I am good at, tumbling
I love to tumble,
I am also good at stunting too
Every year we go to competitions a lot.
Most of mine are in Salt Lake City
Summit is in Orlando, Florida.
I am really good at cheerleading
And I love the cheer uniforms,
And hair, and make up
I also love the shoes,
I love cheer
I am a cheerleader.

Stars
by Isabelle Gonzales

Stars
Glowing, showing
Flying, shining, gliding
Happy– maybe still glowing
Stars

Gymnastics
by Keely Flannery

Gymnastics
I focus, I'm balancing
It's automatic acrobatics
I'm so enthusiastic
Flipping, flying, soaring
It's so graphic
My gymnastics
The way I move I look elastic
Gymnastics so fantastic

My Cool School
by Alexandra Whitlock

Roses are red
Violets are blue,
I am so lucky to have you.
We work and pray,
And play once a day.
St Jerome's School is the best,
I must confess.
We learn all the time,
Increasing our minds.
Friendships I have formed,
Friends I have a swarm.
I enjoy every day,
In this school I wish to stay.
Some days we laugh and some days we cry,
I am here for you with a tissue for your eyes to dry,
An encouraging word, friendly smile or a hug,
Will help to get rid of that sad or mean mug.
I am so blessed even though I have to wear a uniform I guess.
My school family stands above the rest ...

My Life As a Queen
by Paola Trapani

I am moonbeam.
I like to relax in the sun.
I eat the sunbeams by turning them into sugar.
I have a happy life in the sun.
At night, I go deep down into my roots and go to sleep.
My favorite color is hot pink!
I stand tall as the queen.
I see all the bushes and trees that guard me.

What If
by Laykin Valles

What if superheroes were real?
I might yearn to be one!
What if ice cream could stop heart disease?
I would be a medical doctor for that!
What if clocks were time machines?
I would go to Abe Lincoln's house!
What is dreams can come true?
I can wish anything I want!

What You Are Is ...
by Adilyn Sturges

To: Mrs. Fontenot
What you are is ...
Welcome back to the classroom. I've missed you very much.
It is like you're the sun and I am Mercury and everyone else is the other planets.
So, without you , we would be lost. Literally.
PS. It's a beautiful day and I can't stop myself from smiling
PSS. You're very beautiful.
I just want you to know that you are very special to us, special to me
and if you know me very good, you would know I'm not lying
because you're like in my family and even if I move to Idaho,
I will never ever forget you.
You're like sun and I'm rain, me without you wouldn't make a rainbow.
Sincerely,
Adilyn Kaidie Sturges

Sunflower
by Nakiah Miles

sunflower
yellow, flower
planting, growing, watering
hot– sitting in sun.
Sunflower

Growing
by Emily McDonough

We are growing, so is he,
She is spouting happily,
So very happily!
The teacher teaches reading,
And she teaches writing.
And we find it very exciting!!

Happiness
by Meady Chiem

As the sun rises up,
wonders of joy, appears in the sunlight.
The sound of laughter, warms my heart.
As the butterflies, moths, and hummingbirds,
sing and dance all day,
while I prance around in the wet grass.
Happiness can come from great success,
or it might come from family and friends.
Happiness comes within.
It is a feeling, an emotion,
something that cannot be bought.
Life is short.
You must treasure it because,
whatever you decide to do,
make sure it makes you happy.

Riding My Bike
by Andrew Orapallo

Riding my bike is fun
I raced my friend and won
I ride it in the rain
I ride it through the mud
I ride it till my legs ache with pain
I ride my bike with my cousins
We ride all over my neighborhood
Sometimes we are loud, but we are always good
We ride all day and night
We ride until we are out of sight
We ride on trails and over rocks
We ride to the river and over docks
We ride to parks and through the streams
I even ride my bike in my dreams

Lion's Roar
by Rachel Sokolowski

It's so loud I can hear it from miles away.
I get closer to the noise.
I look through the bushes.
I see standing there a beautiful lion, graceful and majestic.
He roars again, this time louder.
He sees me in the bushes.
He is staring at me and I am staring back.
His coat smooth and fine.
His piercing gold eyes glisten in the sun.
He walks toward me.
I emerge from the bushes into the light.
We are standing next to each other.
He brushes against my arm as I softly stroke his back.
His fur like silk.
He sits in front of me and roars.
He rolls over playfully and purrs happily as I stroke him again.
I hear another loud roar.
This time coming from one of his pack.
He stands, looks at me and runs back to his pride.

Angels
by Lindsay Ujobai

Beautiful creatures that watch over everyone.
Everyone has an astounding angel watching them.
Evil or good, everyone has a remarkable angel watching over them.
Angels watch over me and you every night.

Today Is a New Day!
by Lily Barzousky

Today is a new day! Get up and play.
Have a ball, dance and play.
Sing a song, leap and say, "Hurray for the day!"
Today is a new day!
Play outside, laugh out loud,
Be a friend, find something to mend.
Read a book, learn to cook,
Paint a mural and break a rule!
Today is a new day!
Let cares and worries go away.
Be the best you, you can be,
and say, "Thank You, Lord, for making me, me!"

That Big Old Tree
by Emily Dougherty

That big old tree sits there,
It is as strong as a horse,
It doesn't move an inch,
No, it just sits there.
That big old tree has a lot,
Though it doesn't move an inch,
No, it just sits there.
Oh, that tree gets older every day,
Season by season, tornado by hurricane,
It just sits there.
Even winter, summer, spring, and fall can't knock that old tree down
Oh, that tree just sits there,
Getting passed by all day,
It just sits there.

Cluck the Duck
by Luke DiBricida

There was once a duck,
His name was Cluck,
His brother's name was Buck who had a truck,
They drove the truck into the muck,
They had no luck,
Cluck started to yell at Buck,
They couldn't get the truck out of the muck,
Then Cluck saw Daddy Duck,
Daddy Duck pulled the truck out of the muck,
Buck said, "Thank you, Daddy Duck,"
"Daddy Duck has lots of luck," says Cluck,
"You're right, Cluck," said Buck,
"Let's have dinner," said Mother Duck

Freedom
by Liam Schmidt

Oh how great it is to be free.
Freedom for you,
Freedom for me.
A country, a state,
A city, a home,
A nice place to call our own.
No one's a slave,
All can vote,
Write anything on a note.
No kings to tell us what to do,
Freedom for me,
Freedom for you.
Though we're free we have some rules.
No killing, speeding, or stealing jewels.
So throw a party,
Go to a ball,
Freedom for one,
Freedom for all.

The Exciting Journey
by Benjamin Fall

The park is quiet, peaceful as can be.
Trying to get close to the nice daughter
As I walk on the path made from a tree
I see a stream of nice flowing water
Going to the water happy to see
What is in store for us all together
Running and running to find lots of glee
Seeing many beautiful blue feathers
Picking at grass, playing some awesome tag.
Looking for a giant playground to play
Trying to find many giant soft rags
To cool us off in the beautiful day
As the friends are growing much more friendly
I see the park is exciting to me!

Oh, By the Seaside
by Devyn Stek

Oh, by the seaside
The waves crashing
Fierce as can be
Oh, by the seaside
The wind blowing
With all its might
Oh, by the seaside
With the heat growing heavy
Summer rains bring relief
Oh, by the seaside
Children laughing and playing
With friends
Oh, by the seaside
That wonderful seaside
Is home to me
And is where
I belong

Old Man
by Ethan Dunham

That old man is so funny
He has a very fat bunny
The old man jumps
The bunny has lumps
Oh isn't it so funny

My Psalm To God
by Cameron Davis

Where can I hide from you, God?
If I went to the bottom of the sea, You would be there with me.
If I went to the farthest star, You would be by my side.
If I went to the highest Heavens, You would be guiding me there.
If I was in the darkest part of the world, You would be my light.
If I were to be in the worst place in the world, You would be my happiness.
Love,
Cameron

Spring Is Here
by Ashley Mitchell

Spring is here
Listen to us cheer
Flowers will bloom and blossom
Dogs will play, how awesome
We love to run and play
Yes, we'll have some fun today
The day is bright
Not like night
Grass will be green
Nobody will be mean
The skies are blue
I know that's true
Everything is very wet
It's not summer yet
Spring is great
But it's not too late
Seeds will sprout
And children will shout
Oh spring is here!
Oh spring is here!

Giving
by Kaleb Ricks

Giving
Share, help
Caring, assist, hand out
Giving people gifts
Nice

Lydia Darragh
by Casey Ashcraft

Lydia Darragh was a Patriot spy
British officers using her home, made her want to cry.
They used one room to discuss their plan,
Planning to attack in two days on General Washington.
Lydia overheard and wrote a note.
The Americans prepared and went to devote,
They were ready to defeat,
The British called for a retreat.

Misty My Hamster
by Amber Cram

Misty, oh Misty, my dear dear Misty
your fur
is soft and smooth
your eyes are shining
blue
and your ears are
black and white
while you waddle
away
in the sun
you are a
very
good friend but
you do know
you don't smell so
well

It's Their Life
by Paige Greenwell

No one cry, it's just a fly
It's a fly's life.
No one weep, it's just a sheep.
It's a sheep's life.
Don't you dare, it's my mare!
She's my life.

Silly
by Ella Clark

I don't know what to write for poem
So I might as well stay home
I am going to pretend I am sick today
But later I am going out to play
I don't want to write a silly poem
I would rather run to Nome

My Dad
by Wyatt Christensen

My dad is so fun
He takes me outside to play and run,
He even knows how to shoot a gun,
When he talks to my mom
He calls her "Hun,"
He even loves to spend time with his only son.

The River Bay
by Hannah Schmidt

The sound of the river bay relaxes me.
As I can put my thoughts to mind.
It brings my memories to life, as I relive them.
I remember friends and my family.
I hear them laugh and see them play by the river bay.
When I am alone by the river bay.
I feel happy and comforted.
That is the sound of the river bay.

Flowers Getting Showers
by Vanessa Hoene

I see pretty flowers
taking showers
flowers are so pretty
they make me giddy
when you plant a seed
you are doing a good deed
because bees need honey
and it is like money
that is why there are flowers everywhere
more than enough to share

My Room
by Sierra Sedeno

My room is the only place to go,
When I need some peace and quiet.
Or when I want to listen to music or even stare into space.
When I want to play games or read a book.
I can plop on my bed and sleep like a baby.
I can snuggle in my warm blanket.
I can do my homework and then relax.
All I have to do is look and say ....
What am I going to do today?

Wolves
by Brendan Dadourian

Wolves, wolves, oh how I love wolves!
Wolves are stealthy
Wolves are dangerous
Wolves are smooth
Wolves stalk their prey
Their teeth are huge
Wolves are fierce
And wolves are sly
Wolves are like wild dogs
And they are scary
If you see one you'll probably run
But the way I see them
Wolves are awesome
Wolves, wolves, oh how I love wolves!

Black Cat
by Ashley Strunk

I fling my cat tail all around with the black cat army at the graveyard
I prowl and hunt for birds and mice through the grass at the graveyard
I hear a dog howling at the moon, I look, oh snap, it's right there
I let out a shriek, we head for the street, the dog is following behind us
The street lights are lit, the pumpkins are lit, nowhere to go but the forest
I climb up a tree where no one can see me, climb down, go to the graveyard.

Synergize
by Anjoelina Sauceda

The habit synergize is not about lies.
Or about silly little baby cries.
The habit synergize is mostly about being a great team.
So nothing will come out of people's ears like steam.
If you want to be a wonderful leader you have to work in a group.
You don't need to worry because it will all seem just like a dream to you and me.
Synergizing is like a friendly bumblebee.
It will never ever hurt anyone's feelings.
If a leader can synergize then you can synergize just like them.
Remember the choices you make today are shaping the leader in you.

How To Be a Princess
by Hannah Rozenbaum

To be a princess you have to be sweet and kind and promise not to lose your mind.
To be a princess you have to be smart. You can't just be a master of art.
To be a princess you have to smile, you can't just have a lot of style.
To be a princess you can't be shy and you definitely cannot cry.
To be princess you must not shout or someone will definitely kick you out.
To be a princess you must be prepared and not at all scared.
To be a princess you must have gold. Well, at least that's what I've been told.
To be a princess you need to forget bad days even if there are no ways.
To be a princess you can't have a gun and you must know how to have some fun.
Now that you know what princesses do, you can be a princess too.

Ice Hockey Rink
by D'Mar McCoy

In the hockey rink, a day with fans cheering their voices off.
The smell of hot dogs, pizza, pretzels, and fries smacks your nose
with a powerful scent when you walk past the snack bar.
A high paced game with speed and power starts like a flashing lightning bolt.
"Slap shots roar with anger, shouting a thundering roar,
Get out of my way, POW, BANG, and BOOM."
Loud horns, and bells say, "Go team, go," with joy, and love.
At the end of the game a demanding horn says,
"Get off the ice," like it is the king of the rink.
Then happiness, joy, and glee rushes down to the winning team to congratulate them.
Next sorrow, sadness, and anger runs to the losing team to make fun of them.

Spring
by Keira Albert

Spring is here!
It is filled with cheer!
People sing.
Even the bees that sting.
Spring is here!
It is filled with cheer!
Some people dance.
Others take a chance.
Plants grow.
Trees too, but slow.
Grass is green.
People are not mean.
Spring is here!
It is filled with cheer!
Many people feel the same:
Spring is here, it finally came!
People shop.
Some never stop.
Spring is here!
It is filled with cheer!

Spring Fling
by Elloise Hellyer

Spring is a fling
You can win a wing
Flowers grow off things
The only problem is testing you have to do

Feather
by Samuel Miller

A light little thing
Gliding across the air
In a wistful motion,
The gentle spring breeze making it fly
Like a living thing.
Fuzzy, hairy and many more,
Plucked from a bird.
I set it free,
I let the wind take it.
Watching it fly away
To wherever it wants to go.

Mysteries
by Sarah Zhang

"Shhh!" You shush,
"I found a clue in this bush!"
Tip-toe down the narrow stairs,
Seeking for the evil heir.
"It's over here!"
"No! It's over there!"
Slip into a dark suit,
Make sure you're on absolute mute.
Focus on your quest,
And not on the rest.
The floorboard goes CREAK!
You quiver, but you take a peek.
"Nothing here."
"Nothing there."
You will not give up, and before you know it,
You did it.
You found the evil heir,
And he was hiding in a box, I think it was over there.

Talking To People
by Bree Anderson

Bree's here
What is your name?
"Beth," Beth, I like that name
Can you get some books to my house?
Yes. Bye.

Wolves
by Aurora Grace Marks

Howling at the moon.
Paws pounding at the earth,
Chasing deer, moose, and elk
Catching prey for dinner.
Big, grey, and muscular,
Growling at strays.
Sleeping in a pack,
With friends.

Cemetery
by Erin Eddy

The graves mark the winding path through the dead,
shadowy figures glissade behind you.
An ear piercing scream fills the air
apple red blood covers the worn dirt path.
Night stealthily sneaks upon you,
without much thought you start to run
your breathing races,
the cold air tastes bitter,
your eyes sting
a spine chilling BOOM! erupts.
A cloaked figure is pursing you,
the secret face beyond the cloak remains unveiled.
Fog hovers just above the ground
the downcast and miserable place hides grim secrets.
A series of macabre witches cackle overhead
the ominous blackness hides many unknown mysteries.
Tree branches rustle overhead,
your heart's pounding hard enough to burst through your chest
an undetermined object flies out of nowhere,
then … the world goes black …

The Cow That Said Meow
by Clayton Moore

There was a cow
That often said meow
Lots of people said wow
But often said how
They said it was impossible
When they tried to stop him
They often ended up in the hospital

It Is Spring
by Kathleen Le

Say hello to March, April and May
It is already spring today
In spring there is a lot of rain
That is what April contains
The spring, mostly everything is green
That is why March is supreme
In spring, there are always showers
Rain is what makes beautiful May flowers
These are the great spring season
How about a spring celebration

The Meaning of Friendship
by Isabella Zelmanoff

Friendship is a feeling when you are warm and happy inside,
when you feel relaxed, loved and safe with them.
True friendship is when you feel sad and they are right beside you,
being your best friend.
They smile when you smile and, feel the pain when you do,
and when you cry a single tear, they promise they'll cry too!
True friendship is, no backstabbing, and no tattletaling,
and when there are fights they will always come back,
And this is all true!

Skipping
by Carly Futrick

The moonlight twinkles over the water,
that ripples softly in the distance.
A gentle breeze flows through my hair,
and wafts salty air as it passes.
A stony path leads to the water,
that is where the fun begins.
When I take off my pack I find a rock,
that I pick up and toss into the water.
It skips and skips making a trail of its glory as it passes,
Until with a CLUNK the tiny pebble sinks into the water,
It swims and swims farther under,
to meet the other rocks whose journeys were identical.
Pebble after pebble their journey ends similar,
the rise and fall of these pebbles isn't always the same.
It's all about luck, skill, patience, and a little bit of practice,
But if their story wasn't so similar,
the tricky game of rocks wouldn't be so satisfying.

I Am From
by Taniya Smith

I am from a long line of generations of Mary.
I am from my nickname Tiny Mary because I am the youngest
and I look like my mom.
I am from wondering what I will do for my nephew for his 1st birthday party.
I am from my dreams of what my career is going to be.
I am from my most prized possession is my dog that I will always love,
even in Paris.
I am from my neighborhood that is loud at night and quiet during the day.
I am from the things I hear when I'm on my block: a lot of shouting.
I am from my fears when I hear scary stories.
I am from my values. What I believe in is trust.
I am from my hair that's as soft as a pillow.
I am from loving candy and anything sweet and tasty.

Friends
by Sami Bissey

Friends are there when you cry.
Friends are there when you are shy.
You have good friends by your side.
They make you laugh and fill you with pride
You always have them in your heart
You and your best friend should never be apart.
You are perfect as perfect can be.
A friend like you will never leave me.

My Own Star
by Sophia Lavigna

One starry night, I looked outside,
there were millions of stars dancing through the sky,
but there was one, that one special star, that was looking down at me.
I saw it smile, but I had to blink twice.
Was it real? did it really smile at me? was all that went through my mind.
I looked back up and there was that star, still, smiling as bright as the sun.
I took out my camera and took a picture,
but when I looked at it, it was as blank as the sky without stars.
I decided I would take a mental picture,
even though I already knew I would never forget that one special star.
I went inside and looked out my window,
and there was that star, still smiling down at me.
I went to bed and when the next night came, there was that one special star.
I saw it moving, not just back in forth, but in a special way,
like it was trying to tell me something by using code.
As I figured it out, it was trying to tell me that it was my star.
That star told me it was my star, but I still wasn't sure what that meant.
How was it my star, a star just for me, but as I was thinking I saw something happen.
Not only my star, but all the others, started to dance in one special way.
But then I saw it, a one of a kind star, floating across the dancing stars,
but at lightning speed.
Then I realized it was a shooting star, I made a wish, one very special wish.
My wish you may ask, well it already came true,
that that one special star would never go away.
That was when I was a little girl, but this is now, 50 years into the future.
But I'm still watching that special star, with a smile that went from the North Pole,
to the South Pole on one starry night.

The Three Talented Birds
by Yamil Perez

The three talented birds
An owl can hoot
A parrot can play the flute
And a penguin can use a parachute!

Waves
by Genevieve Savage

Erase footprints of fallen waves,
as they wash over the sand, very tame.
Running back and forth ... Never quite the same.
Bumpy, curvy, looking kinda like steed.
Whenever you race it, it's always in the lead.
The sun shines and reflects with light.
It's so perfect ... just right.
The shadows creep over the salty, foamy, slick water,
never quite the same rhythm.
Lonely water travels down,
tickling toes.
I hope the waves will never stop ... but really,
Who knows?

Rainbow
by Kate Malandra

A big white and gray cotton candy piece is in the sky
Tears start coming from the cotton candy.
First 1 tear, then 2 tears, then 3 tears.
Suddenly more than 10,000 tears come down,
It starts as seconds, then minutes, then hours.
Finally it was slowing down
From hours, to minutes, to seconds,
Now the cotton candy is whimpering,
Suddenly a beautiful, colorful, bridge appears,
It's red, orange, yellow, green, blue, indigo, and violet.
Time flies by, and an hour has gone by
Now the bridge starts fading away ...
POOF! It's gone.
Now all I see is pure white cotton candy in the sky,
One piece looks like a snake.

Expedition
by Alison Yang

Expedition
Very excited
Hardships along the way
Made it to the Pacific
Going home

Failed
by Jade Miller

We're the people who create, then you kill each other like live bait
You say you'll never hurt them, then you desert them
Then there you are in a cell thinking about how you failed
After five years you finally make bail, you're out of jail
You go back home and your cousins are fussing
Then you start with drugs and then you get addicted to alcohol
You got back to your old ways, then you see yourself in a cell, you say
"My life was terrible and I FAILED"

Springtime
by LoRon Pearson

With all of its beauty
and all spectacular sights,
it's springtime at last
with all its pretty heights.
All of the blooming flowers
and all of the blossom trees
lots of insects flying around
including honey bees.
The sweet taste of red apples
the honey from the tree bark
the wet dew on the grass
and the kids up at the park.
Spring is finally here!
Just feel the breeze in your hair.
It might be spring here,
but to me spring is everywhere

Spring Is In the Air
by Alivia Castillo

Tulips and roses are blooming
The leaves on the trees are growing back
Because spring is in the air

The Beautiful Savanna
by John McLaughlin

I want to see the savanna one day,
so I can see the beautiful animals at play.
The baboons playing in the sun,
the hyenas laughing and having fun,
cheetahs running by fast
and the large elephants watching them go past.
I see giraffes reaching for the large trees
and rhino's wrinkly knees.
The zebra so fashionable with their stripes
and the lions so fierce with their might!
Oh this beautiful place,
I wish I could see it with my own face.

I Am
by Edgar Nunez

I am a football fan and a Seahawks fan
I wonder if they know I play football
I hear a coach blowing his whistle in a football field
I see the ball back and forth
I want a football signed by my favorite player
I am a football fan and a Seahawks fan
I pretend I win the game tomorrow
I feel glad when we win the game
I touch the football when they throw it at me
I worry about messing up in the game
I cry when we win the game and people are cheering
I am a football fan and a Seahawks fan
I understand when we lose it is not their fault
I say good luck when the game starts
I dream of being an NFL player
I try being the best on my team

The Art of Love
by Logan Kaylor

We stand in the moonlight all alone,
In her eyes at last I am at home.
Everything is still just for us,
Then I realize that I must.
I close my eyes and kiss her there,
A special moment that we share.
Love can be wonderful if they offer their soul,
making you realize you never were whole.
Or love can bind you in a yearning chain,
that offers nothing more than endless pain.
In the end it's all a big gamble of
heart for heart– the art of love.

I Am Lexis
by Lexis Wayenberg

I am adventurous and nice
I wonder about how the world works
I hear my voice questioning about everything
I see the waterfall crashing onto the rocks
I want to see my family together again
I am adventurous and nice
I pretend that I am magical
I feel amazed about how nice people can be
I touch the stars in the sky
I worry about my friends
I cry when I feel alone
I am adventurous and nice
I understand that life's not fair
I say don't cry over spilt milk
I dream about owning my own bakery
across from my friend's pet rescue center
I try to be myself
I hope I will have an optimistic life
I am adventurous and nice

Rain and Wind
by Sydnee Brown

On the rainy day
Rain touches my paper
Wind blows my paper away
Oh crap, I need that back

Skating
by Kelly Grable

When I skate
I feel just great.
When I fall, I try again.
Then I improve
My spins and moves.
When I spin
I always grin
Because people are shouting. Wow!
So try to skate
And you'll feel great.

Greek Mythology
by Lindsey Crandall

Icarus stumbled off the cliff
Only to straighten out, and start to drift
He enjoyed the feeling so he flew up,
But his wings had melted rather abrupt
Calypso had chosen the wrong side
She was punished by being wakened by the tide
She couldn't leave, she was immortal, and boys were sent
She fell in love, but they had to go, time past and went
Narcissus was an extremely pretty boy
But a girl named Echo was annoyed
She told him to stop looking at himself, but she couldn't speak
She was cursed by Hera, and Narcissus didn't eat, he was very bleak
Out of all of Chiron's brethren, he was the only one
Who sacrificed his time so great things could be done
He trained his heroes to fight like a pro
So they could defeat the monsters that were foes
Now that you've a few short stories, what do you think?
Do you know the lesson overall? All of them have a link
Greek Mythology is fun to learn
Now that you like it, why don't you take a turn?

Summertime
by Madison O'Malley

Summer is here,
It's time to play,
Birds are chirping,
Kids are playing,
Laughter is coming,
Flowers are blooming,
Summer is here!

Trees
by Jennah Bolden

Everywhere you go you see trees,
They are brown and green, and have leaves,
The leaves change in winter and fall,
They're also really tall,
Trees are hard and rough,
They are also very tough,
Trees give you allergies,
They can also make you sneeze,
In winter they usually lose their leaves,
Isn't this stuff so amazing about trees,

A Week In a Rain Forest
by Evan Seklecki

Birds, monkeys, trees
not as loud as the bright leaves.
Moist, hot, loud, "GROWL"
I'm hearing the sound of the jaguar now,
It's getting dark should I stay or should I go,
The sounds of a cricket tell me no,
The sun rises, it's a beautiful day,
the gentle breeze is blowing every way.
It has been one amazing April afternoon,
slowly and slowly the flowers bloom,
I'm just sitting here trying to draw this eastern waterfall.
Yes there is plenty of rain forests to draw, but this is the best of all.

A Trip To the Jungle
by Amiera Forbes

Monkeys swing from tree to tree,
The grass is green as can be,
Flowers dancing peacefully.
The tigers' roar frightened me,
Beautiful butterflies following me,
Oh, how pretty the jungle can be!

What To Do In Philadelphia, PA
by Luis Pacheco

Go to ShopRite, buy avocados
Count cigarettes on the floor
Head to Oteri's, buy cannoli
Watch the police go by
Count twenty people who've never been here
Go to the mall, count the coins in the fountain
Guess how many people live here
Then go eat a cheesesteak

The Men Who Serve
by Dean Bergkoetter

Thank you military men who risk your lives for us,
I know I can give you all my trust.
I know you don't do it just for me,
But for all the people in the world we see.
So I should do you a favor,
I don't know what to do,
I know it must be for you,
Hmmm, this feels like déjà vu.
I thought of this before,
I don't know what to do,
I'll send you packages,
Especially just for you.

Dog In France
by Alexis Law

There once was a dog in France
Who needed to buy some new pants
He wanted to fly
But didn't know why
So, instead he took up dance.

Why You Eat My Pie?
by Xzander Omundson

I love pie.
It's delicious, no lie.
It tastes so fine.
It's better than fries.
You ate my pie!
I think I'll cry.
I would cry but I'm just too shy.
I'll just die.
I'll just eat this fly.
Or at least I'll try.
What am I talking about? There's pie I can buy.
I'll eat it and there you shall I lie.

Different Beats On the Street
by Tyliah Smith

The music is perfect
It's really worth it
I love to hear my favorite jam
It makes me want to go slam and jam
Music is on the street
Because I hear my favorite beat
I hear the birds chirping
Animals have a lot of music
They've always used it
Babies have perfect harmony
When they cry
Even when they sigh
On the streets I hear different beats
I think if you put music to the test
Trust me it will be the best
The beats are on the streets

Reeses
by Fiorella Garcia

There once was a young girl named Reeses
who happened to love eating peeses
she ate them all day
in the most messy way
But still found time to get leeses.

What's the Matter With Our Team?
by Isabel Wallacavage

Dear oh dear, what's the matter with our team?
No longer does steam cloud around them as they run,
oh our team, our team.
It's as though our coach turned into a cockroach!
(Ahem, did you actually look?)
Oh no! Our coach really is a cockroach!

I Am
by Sibylle Beltran-Grémaud

I am friendly and kind
I wonder how this life would be without me.
I hear the sun speaking
I see imaginary animals.
I want peace in all the world.
I am friendly and kind.
I pretend trees and animals can talk our language.
I feel the warm wind touching my face.
I worry about the animals in danger.
I cry when something is very sad.
I am friendly and kind.
I understand that nothing is fair.
I say, "I'll do my best."
I dream of people all around the world.
I try saving the Earth by recycling and composting.
I hope people would live happily.
I am friendly and kind.

Peace and Love
by Sofia Petrone

Peace is love
Peace is you and me
Peace is anybody
Peace is time travel
The whole world is peace, peace, peace, peace.
Peace runs through the air
Peace and love are everywhere.
It might not seem like it but you just do not know it yet.
Love and peace are bam, thump, zipp, buzz.
Peace and love are awesome
Peace, peace, peace, love, love, love.
I love peace and love,
and love, love, love, peace, peace, peace
Peace and love.

New Prospects
by Jessica Schneider

I got in a fight, it just wasn't fair.
It wasn't my fault! But why should they care?
I needed to go, but I didn't know how.
Should I wait for a bit, or should I go now?
I ran from home, without a care.
I stormed away; I needed new air.
But they don't understand, or know how I feel.
And so I just walked, my anger so real.
What is that meadow, just over there?
I went inside, as far as I'd dare.
Around and around, I ran and I twirled.
Away from my feelings, away from the world.
I couldn't just hide, soon I did find.
So I headed out, with new prospects in mind.
I walked out with a new spring in my step.
I was ready to face the world again.

Peace
by Rosalie Kraines

The smell of cherry water ice,
the waves lapping the shore,
like a cat laps its milk.
Watching the sun go down,
bringing the moon up.
Seeing the stars form constellations,
listening to old myths about Rome,
whispering about gentile things,
for instance, nature.
Playing the piano,
reading fantasy on the couch,
hearing trees sway gently,
in the wind.
Leaves rustling about,
everywhere.
Content and,
dreaming about peace.

Magic of the World
by Vir Acharya

Our world
has so many mysteries
and magic
magic in the animals
the plants
and all of nature
magic in all of us
in me and you
magic in every inch of the Earth
this beautiful world
keeps us alive
keeps us breathing
keeps us reaching
reaching for the stars
to grab a new magic
and bring it to this world
this magical world

Elements of Life
by Sarah Wong

Ice can shatter easily
but ice can also reflect
fire can burn away your love
but fire can protect
both are enemies and friends
of every side beyond
Water drowns your hope
and creates beauty in one pond
air can blow away your heart
but makes your breathing bond
To your body

Hopes and Dreams
by Christina Lu

Is hope the only thing that keeps your life going?
You dream about getting things that look awesome,
like getting a BMX, Xbox One, new house, latest technologies,
or even the best grades, but that's just hope.
Throwing your hope in the wishing well? Nice, but that will just make you mope.
In the spotlight, in reality, you should be the person who is glowing!
Don't dream it, but go for your hope, chase after it to make sure it comes true!
Your world is all about the main character in reality, you.
What do you think is hope?
I think hope is just a life where people can count on or believe
because you can just go for it without dreaming.
Let everyone see your achievement and your face beaming.
Would you want someone to take your hopes and dreams away?
No, nobody tells the main character what to do
because you are the person who is supposed to make the decisions in your life!
Someone wants you to leave, but you want to stay.
Reality has disagreements and strifes.
People trying to make do the things they wanted to do when they were young.
They want to brag to their friends about your achievements.
Do you want to close your hopes with a bung.
Just make the people who you love love, but is dead
other than just making a bereavement.
So stop dreaming and go for your goal!
Don't let anybody control your future
because they aren't the main characters in your story.
Every family wants their children to have a lot of dole.
People just want to steal your glory

The Kid On My Block
by Joshua Lai

There's a kid on my block
that really likes trees.
When he goes to the doc
he sings about me.
That kid likes the beach
as you can scc.
I hate it when
he sings about me.

Music
by Sierra Church

Music is everywhere,
Music is my life.
If it was a person,
I would ask it to be my wife.
Music is a story,
Something someone tells you.
It can be about the bright green grass,
Or the sky which is blue.

Winners?
by Kerry Lopez

This week is our final game!
"Do you think we'll do fine?"
Said our teammate Zane.
Maybe? It seems they haven't lost since 1779!
"The Machines!"
Said Lain
They are such a good team.
I hope we win, I won't want to feel the pain.
"Don't worry," said Tim
We'll spy on them and see how they play.
It's an idea that we'll for sure win
So we know what to expect that day
And then at night we'll change the posts
And when we play we'll roam the field.
See I told you we would win the game!
But it always didn't feel the same.

Storm
by Dayton Grover

Something someone sometimes loves
Thunder like a drum plays the beat of the night
Out of nowhere it appears like a light in the air
Rumbles through the sky on a sea up high
Mumbles something no one knows, but every word is heard

Mtn View Bengals
by Ivy Rayburn

Most cool
Tigers
Never lose

Very awesome
Interesting
Excited every day of the year
We never give up

Bengal tigers
Enjoy winning
Nice to competitors
Always there for each other
Great at sports
Losing isn't an option
Sophisticated

100
by Tristan Prosper

I can handle 100 hands
I could run up 100 stands
up down ... up ... down ...
I could eat 100 cakes
But I couldn't swim in 100 lakes
I could have 100 noses
with those I could smell 100 roses
I could have 100 blisters
But I wouldn't– I repeat– would not want 100 sisters
I could have 100 dishes
I could have 100 fishes (has to be salmon)
I could have 100 toes
But I could NOT I mean NOT have 100 "Let it Go's"

Stargazing
by Allison Arnold

Little lights shine in the dark night sky,
See one, see two, see many bright stars and wonders pass by.
A bright moon seems to control the endless space,
As we lay on our backs and watch, having no pace
The sun has gone in hibernation for when the daytime starts to peel,
Stars come out of their hiding and light the sky with feel.
Soon the sun comes out again and leaves the sky to day,
But for now when the sky is black, we will gaze at the stars and lay.

Feelings Change
by D'Nyah Jefferson-Philmore

T
  E   Life-Threatening
    A
     R
      S
  Tears, Tears   Bullying
  People pushing
  You   around
 calling   you   names.

  you just stand   there, Heavyhearted
       Defenseless
 letting it   all   happen.
  A   few   seconds   later   Outcast
 you're in the janitor's closet
       crying.   Intimidated

  no   one stands up   for   you
 They   think   you're a   JOKE
 Next   thing you   know,
  you're   running   home Alone
  after school, as fast as
   a cheetah, mind racing,
   repeating   the day
    over and over
    Asking,
   Why did they pick
   ME!

I Am
by Eleonore Perrigueur

I am a girl who likes nature and animals.
I wonder if I will see a wild animal.
I hear the wind breathe.
I see the nature move.
I want to have an animal.
I am a girl who likes nature and animals.
I pretend to see animals around me.
I feel the grass on my feet.
I touch the biggest tree of the forest.
I worry I never see animals.
I cry to not have one.
I am a girl who likes nature and animals.
I understand that they don't want to be shown.
I say that they need to have liberty.
I dream the word.
I try to recycle things.
I hope that I would see a wild animal.
I am a girl who likes nature and animals.

A Country For All
by Asher Donohue

When I hear the famous words
So many Americans love
I do not feel the freedom
That our forefathers spoke of.
They said, "All men are equal
And deserve to pursue happiness"
But in my mind I see slave ships
Full of broken souls and hopelessness
And as those patriots penned
The words that formed our laws
I see black slaves at work
And I see our country's flaws.
But through long years of toil
That hateful practice diminished
Courageous leaders gave their lives
And slavery was finished.
And now in colorful harmony
Both races live as one
Sharing our great country
Underneath this bright broad sun.

The Car
by Baptiste Reliquet

Once there was a car
She went to the bar
She found an oven
Inside she found a dragon
She was scared because it was a band
Then she found sand
It was a beach
Where there was a peach
She had to go
She went to her house
She saw a mouse
So she ran away

The Moon
by Layth Bromgard

The moon has no air.
And the moon has big holes in it.
The moon can Disappear.
And the moon can be very dangerous.
the moon is very scary.
Always take a space helmet to space.

The Mysterious Spring
by Cristina Burz

The sun shines on the flowers after the rain pattered on my house
Whenever I go in the field the grass is soft
and scrambling around is that one field mouse
The trees sway to and fro
Then there is that house were the flowers never grow
A house where the sun never shines
The house filled with vines
The moon light shimmers at night
And its so bright
I go outside and look at the moon
I look at the house then the moon above the tree that grows one prune
And the house is gone

3rd Place

Kaleb Caraway

Born To Fly
by Kaleb Caraway

The time has come for mama to teach her young eaglet how to fly,
Easing him near the edge, she encourages him to try.
As he looks at the world below, fear and doubt arise,
Looking for assurance, he searches his mother's eyes.
Mother gently pushes him, her pride she can't deny,
This is your day, my child, you were born to fly.
You were born, you were born to fly,
On the wind of my spirit, you will soar above the sky.
Stretch your wings, now is the time,
You are ready, you were born to fly.

2nd Place

Samantha Cake

Elephants Running
by Samantha Cake

At first only raindrops in the distance,
Then a ravenous thunderstorm ranting,
It evolves into boulders falling from the sky.
Elephants are running.
With fire in their hearts burning,
They stampede over the dry earth.
Dark eyes with compassion inlaid,
Focused on the rising sun,
Running and running towards the light.
Muscles flexing with stunning force,
Creating a tsunami of dust
That comes swirling down.
The mighty beasts tear across the savannah,
Blazing a trail in their wake,
Proving that nature is strong with determination.
Shaking the mighty Earth,
Changing the future to come,
Feeling freedom blow across their foreheads.
Loving the world for what it is while running.

Joya Breinholt

With dreams of attending Yale University
and someday being a novelist,
Joya is obviously a very observant 5th grade student
with a descriptive flair.
Her love of nature, as found in her own backyard,
provided the perfect backdrop for her award-winning poem.
Congratulations!

Illustrated City Flower
by Joya Breinholt

The fringed leaves
Of the Japanese maple tree
Are familiar to the little girl
Her auburn brown eyes
Are captured by
An explosion of pink gypsy blossoms
The ticking of the clock
Is as audible as
Old airplane parts
Rusting and rusting
Over centuries and centuries
In the illusion of the sun

Division II

Grades
6-7

Frenemies
by Jade Weber

You say hello, I say hi.
As I stare into your eyes,
I could tell that we would be friends,
But with no lies.
Later on in our lives,
You tell me your brother just died.
Oh, I felt so bad.
Later that day I hear people say,
Did you hear, Lisa lied to Jade?
I ran and hid,
I ran from the rumors spreading fast.
Then finally, a light bulb went off in my head, ding.
I went to go find my friend with the lies,
But no luck to my surprise.
There she goes behind a tree.
I go find her hiding from me.
I tell her, "Instead of friends, I think we are enemies."
She asked me, "Can't we still be friends?"
I said, "Fine, we can be frenemies."
But don't worry, I will still remember the time that,
You said hello, and I said hi.

The Secret Truth of the Plant's Plea
by Sophia Snyder

White lava sputters trying to breathe under the water's glistening surface
before it gets pulled into a writhing cyclone of bubbles
from the spiritual water sprouts a beautiful maple tree
with supple green leaves
they turn red with rage as the seasons change
drenching the attacker with scorching hot magma
The attacker just a simple bee, lands on the beautiful tree
making the tree sway in such a horrific way
with the help of the north wind
under the roots the route is clear
Then they came from everywhere
Bugs! Bugs! Crawl down the walls, a saving plea to the bee
while the tree was thrashing, the bugs were shaken affright
fear splatters plopping from leaf to leaf
covering the once pretty tree forming
condensing the Earth's new face
making it as real as life itself
converting all life anew

Blades Touch the Ice
by Chaney Kirkmire

My blades touch the ice
The snow shining bright
It becomes cloudy
And I hope I can see
My blades touch the ice
I want to fly high
But I forgot I am scared of heights
I want to come down so I can feel
My blades touch the ice
I start to begin in a circle
I become dizzy
I drink water
So I can see my blades touch the ice
I glide across the ice twisting and turning
Stop! I finally see my blades touch the ice

Life and Its Ways
by Zoey Roberts

If it was pouring, the wind howled,
the lightning struck, and the thunder boomed–
it's wet, muddy, and cold.
Then look closer:
the rain's feeding the flowers,
the wind whistles a nice tune,
the boom of the thunder is electrifying
and the strike of lightning is brighter than the moon.
If someone had a bad day,
they cried and moped, and they're angry and confused–
they are depressing.
Then look closer:
their parents are fighting, they're getting bad grades–
so give them a smile, and tell them they'll be okay.
If life didn't have sad, nor problems, nor mad–
life would be perfect.
Then look closer:
nothing is perfect, (not any day)
but remember: you can't have a rainbow,
without a little rain.

Spring In a Nutshell
by Shawn Lelewski

The bees are buzzing
The flowers are blossoming
Here comes the springtime

Trees Live and Die
by Kalwin Schied

bits of scorching sun
radiant on my body as trees tent over me
noise of sensation, water repeated multi times, with water blasting
back laid against the birthplace of the lofty tree
leaves shiver as winds inhale back and forth
soil of trees, brown and dusty
fire over various leaves, slowly dying
roots seeking water under the dry ground
pain of tree is silent, veined of it sucking up
the air not water, both of them are good, but water is
for the veined.

Drowning In Sadness
by Natalie Catalano

The darkness is overpowering. You can't breathe.
It feels like the sadness is going down into your throat and choking you.
All you can do is hope that you will be free soon.
After a while you just can't take it anymore and you need to breathe.
It feels like being trapped underwater.
You have no oxygen and there's nothing you can do about it.
You have so many emotions that you don't know what to do.
You want to cry and you want to say goodbye, but you can't.
You're trapped.
All you can do is hide the emotions inside of you and act like you're fine,
When you're really not.
Even though you're struggling through hard times,
you hide it and say that you're fine,
But people never really know the truth of the inside of you.
You feel like there's no happiness, just a dark hole filled with sadness.
You can't even explain the horrible pain it causes.
People believe you're fine.
They will think that you don't have any problems and you're just like them.
This is what they will believe, because that is what you said.
Isn't it?

Bruno
by Bailey Kennedy

His face as chubby as a pig.
His fur as soft as cotton.
He is so cute like baby kittens,
So colorful like black and brown.
His eyes sparkle like the stars in the sky.
He is my Bruno, my one and only Bruno
He is not just a dog, he is my friend.
He is my one and only puppy.

Titanic, Titanic
by Dylan Rex

Titanic, Titanic,
You were gigantic.
You were built like a tank,
Yet you sank.
Built by the White Star Line,
You were so divine.
The lives that were lost,
In that terrible frost.
You took three years,
Through all the blood, sweat, and tears.
Titanic, Titanic,
You were gigantic

Dream
by Maizee Douglass

As I waltz through the trees, I sing a song throughout the night.
I stumble upon a kingdom and a knight. The knight rides to my side,
grabs my hand and says, "Hold on and get ready for the ride."
I can feel the heartbeat of the horse rise as we pick up speed.
We reach the top point of a lookout and gaze upon the sea,
and watch the sunset reflect out onto the water,
"Oh, what a beautiful sight to see!"
The knight gets down from the horse, reaches for my hand
and we stand out in front of the cliff that stretches out from the land.
He holds my hand in his and locks his eyes with mine
and removes his helmet as he leans his face to mine
and whispers, "Wake up my princess, this is only a dream."
He starts running and we jump into the sea.

Spring
by Raymond Pettyjohn

The blossoms bloom, petals uncurl,
thorns grow as the warm breeze whips by,
and the birds sing the signature of spring is near,
as clay softens, the muck grows,
the water rises, the colors are all clear,
and the lukewarm dew lies at the foot of the mountain.

Elk City
by Hannah Penkert

Elk City, Idaho, is a place I call home.
Endless Billy Joel and taking back roads.
Dorky smiles and never-ending fun.
Elk City, Idaho, is number one.
Log cabins and rednecks, ammo and a gun.
There are millions of ways to have fun.
Driving side-by-sides through the mud and
Wearing camo in the sun.
So, in Elk City, Idaho, a place I call home,
Is where all of my memories roam.

Pro-Skittle Rant
by Matias Crespo

There is a treat.
A scrumptious sweet.
Over the ages,
Kids of all ranges
Have come to love it so.
So much we can't control
When they taste the rainbow,
That great and wonderful glow.
To burgers the greats of America,
Know that these small treats will catch up to ya.
It's hard to beat, this wonderful sweet.
The unparalleled, great-tasting eat:
The Skittle!

Spring Is Here
by Justin Morena

Spring is here
Give some cheer
Flowers bloom, trees grow
Water falls, wind blows
Bees buzz, kids play
Yeah spring is here today!
As the moon has risen in the sky
The sun begins to say goodbye
I love spring because spring
Is prettier than a diamond ring
No need to despair
Because spring is in the air.

Yesterday, Today, and Tomorrow
by Chantel Blanco

Yesterday Bethany Mota was a young caring little girl
who loved being homeschooled,
but felt lonely in the presence of only air.
Yesterday her parents decided to attend Bethany to public school
because Bethany's sister, Brittney Mota, said, "It would be fun."
Yesterday Bethany went to school one day as happy as she could be
her smile as bright as the sun and her personality as beautiful as the sunset.
Yesterday Bethany was being bullied by all the kids,
but Bethany never seemed to care.
She turned her cheek and walked away, the anger grew stronger.
Bethany's cries are like grey skies on a rainy day
Yesterday Bethany was homeschooled again
and she was happy to know that no one would judge her.
Today Bethany Mota is 19 years old and absolutely beautiful
Today she is very famous and travels to meet her fans who love and appreciate her
Today she has her own clothing line at Aéropostale
She also makes YouTube videos to interact with her fans.
Tomorrow she will smile like no other
and have her great personality and earn great accomplishments
Tomorrow she will be as wonderful and bright as she is today

Fangirl
by Emily Peterson

Fangirl
Crazy, passionate
Reading, feeling, crying
I've lived 1000 lives
Knowing, loving, hating
Pain, life
Fandoms

Not Like Shel Silverstein
by Abby Williams

I am not like Shel Silverstein
That much is true to say
And I've got a new assignment today
Write a poem. You've got three days!
Work hard and it will be great
Do your best and put time in
Maybe then you're sure to win
Don't give up, persevere through
Possibly a prize will come to you, come to you
But I am not like Shel Silverstein
That much is true to say …

Spring Flowers
by Ileona Garozzo

Colorful are the flowers
I lay there for hours
There were plenty of rain showers
Then a raspberry bush grew
The grass had dew
There were plants in a shoe
Bees were flying through
Bright is the sun
I played for fun
When I was done
Evening had begun
Spring is here at last!

Life's Mysteries
by Dylan Bjornlie

Lying, wondering
The mysteries life offers
Wishing to know them

Dance
by Julia Atkinson

Dance is fun, dance is great,
You can dance in the sun or in the rain.
When you are sad it will bring you up,
And always make you cheer up!
Since I was young it has been my passion,
And it always has such great fashion.
In dance you can twist and turn,
It's worth the time it takes to learn.
There are different types of dances to learn,
And there are many medals you can earn.
For pointe, there are many rehearsals,
But if you suffer through the pain
You will dance with the professionals.

Gravity
by Graham Haupt

When Jimmy was three
He saw an apple tree
The apple joined his hand
Then it fell like dry sand
Jimmy was confused
He didn't know what he used
His parents weren't home
The only thing there was a garden gnome
He waited and waited for Mom and Dad
If they didn't come, he would be sad
"I'm only 3 years old
Parents not home, now that's cold!"
Then he sees the car pull in
He flails his arm like a fin
He showed his Mom the apple mystery
She said, "Jimmy, that's just gravity."

Daddy
by Cynthia Santos

Daddy
Partner in crime
Forever my hero
I'm his mini-me
Pápi

Time
by Hannah Shaw

It's a 8 line nature rhyme
A rhyme about the leafy time
The freezing time, the too warm time
The time when all's right
Except when you're lost
In the beautiful sight
The sight you see change
Blue, orange, red, violet
Black as night
For it is night

The Battle
by Morgan Hoover

When in battle, two foes do meet
Their armor like the scaly hide
Their swords the claws and fangs
Of the dreadful beast
For when the rivers run red
With the blood needlessly shed,
Two beasts clash
They cut and they slash
Trying their best to beat the other
For when the rivers run red
With the blood needlessly shed,
And as the blood does flow
The victor beats his foe
But everything has a price
For when the rivers run red
With the blood needlessly shed,
The victor has won
But he is scarred for life
And the loser is dead

Trees and Bees
by Jaden Saint-Dic

I like trees
I don't like bees
I like school
I don't like stools
I like peas

Fun Times!
by Giana Sperry

Camping
Running around
Talking to everyone
Making s'mores over the fire
Great fun!

The Man and Cat
by Nicholas Orsini

There was a man
who lived in a can
There was a cat
who had a pet bat
The man's name was Van.

Life Is Great
by Alexa Shull

The peaceful of life
brings me happiness and joy.
Life is more than a game
it's a challenge,
one you need to take on.
I lost a race.
It was a win for me
'cause I finished
Life is wonderful
so embrace it
It can bring you down
but is also amazing
how great it is

Beauty
by Andrea Altobelli

Beauty is all the colors, like a rainbow on a sunny day
It tastes like fruit, all different flavors mixed and matched
It smells like flowers, all unique in their own way
And reminds me of love, with you no matter what
It sounds like society accepting you for who you are
Beauty makes me feel like a fireplace, nice and warm

Emptiness
by Siani Smith

Did you ever feel so
Empty, without a single doubt,
Knowing what it could be,
But couldn't let it out
So full of despair,
Restrained from the air,
With a cover to wear
There was no one to care
So you sat with feelings to spare,
But deep down you had one thought,
Is anyone here to keep me near,
Or have a bit of fullness to share?

Untitled
by Elijah Keck

in the corner of the altar
the statue of Mary looks like
an oasis
a force protecting you from
the demons lurking
outside in the vast desert
the scent of fresh laundry
and garden herbs
permeate the spacious church
surrounding you
like a thick wool blanket
warming you on a
cold dark night

What a Girl Is ...
by Lilly Chhun

A girl ain't a Barbie doll
And she sure don't need your rate
A girl is a queen
Wearing her crown high
And no one tells her what to do
She makes her own decisions
And, boy ... Is a girl powerful
Her heart is warm
But you won't do her harm
A girl is the top of a peak
Standing high above the clouds
A girl is a girl
And nothing can change that
Because she wears her coat proudly

Lost In the Woods
by Erin Fagan

I stare at a creature
It has such a great feature
I don't feel the same
I don't even remember my name
It feels like I'm playing a game
That I can't even claim
I see a sharp weapon
That would aid my protection
I stand there with fear
My destiny was clear
Then I see a flame
Shot with good aim
This is a dragon
Not like the Kraken
A lizard with wings
That looks like it's about to win
I was lost in a piece of writing
It was truly exciting
If I could be lost anywhere
I would want to be there

The Colorful
by Marciella Shallomita

Don't judge a book by its cover
Inside I'm different
Outside I'm different
No one knows which one to judge
Rainbows are colors
Colors are rainbows
We can't see the difference
With the color on our faces
Don't look at the outside
But look at the inside
So don't judge me by how I look outside
Because everyone is different
In their own very special way

The Spring Surprise
by Kylie Shane

Finally, it's actually spring!
I'm going to surprise her with the ring!
I don't think I'm capable of doing it,
I'm going to look like an idiot.
Oh please, help me,
I didn't even plan an entry.
I don't think I have the money,
Oh my, I want to surprise my honey.
Now that I have the ring,
She's going to treat me like a king!
I'm at her house,
She is wearing this beautiful blouse.
I showed her the ring,
She said "It's not worth any bling!"
Apparently, it's not the right flavor,
I told her, "I'm not a mind reader."
You're probably wondering why she ate it,
Because a baker baked it!
Oh yah! Did I forget to mention,
I'm only ten!

My Dad
by Caitlyn Ferguson

My dad has a big head.
He doesn't like to get out of bed.
He is annoying,
And can be quite annoying.
But I love him more than you could have said.

Take Them Off
by Sierra Brooks

I'm going to show the real me
Not the fake behind the glasses
And I'm going to show you what I can do
This is me
And only me
The person behind the glasses
It's time to take them off

Lost
by Ivy Lo

I am lost in your nightmare
I am lost in your daydream
Trapped in your reality
As my own is gone already
I'll show you love but
I'll never realize that you
Treat me like trash
I am wrong when
I think I am right
I lost track of time because
I'm trapped in your mind
I'm wondering if all of my choices
Are right
If my future will be bright
I just can't help myself
But falling in love with you
I just can't realize that
You're not treating me right
I'm lost. I'm lost.

Forest
by Ryan Skeels

The forest so colorful
so green, brown, and yellow
I like to go in the forest because
the color and the view
and to ride my dirt bike
the forest such a good place to ride
good views, and good jumps
The forest, a fun place to ride.

Will Power
by Kepa Guerricabeitia

Birds chirping like choirgirls singing
life fills the air as water fills a glass
love is everlasting as a race with no end
strength is when you're running a race and you can't keep going
strength gave the Israelites will to live in the desert for 40 years
but your will pushes you to win

Simple Gifts
by Caroline Klaiber

As dawn approached, the forest came alive,
From the meager ant to the ferocious bear.
All were awake.
But in the midst of it all, was something small,
Something delicate and graceful,
A butterfly.
As it came,
Its elegantly detailed wings were beating
As if in a rhythm,
Only to stop on my outstretched finger.
It looked at me as if we had a rapport,
As if we shared a history no one else did.
I didn't want this moment to end,
But it did,
Like all good things do.
As the butterfly flew away, deeper into the forest,
I thought to myself,
My simple gift had come and gone.

The Snow
by Levi Morrell

Snow, snow, beautiful snow.
I love your whitened glow.
You are so bright, as bright as moonlight.
I hate to see you go.
My wonderful friend, the snow.

Left Behind
by Noah Makowicz

I search and search
Looking for an island worth taking.
My men are eager for riches and goods.
They want to raid, to capture, to steal.
A sudden yell comes from the starboard deck of the ship,
"Land! Land! Land!"
As we draw closer and closer to the sand,
Everything goes silent
I can only hear the man next to me breathing heavily.
I wait till I'm only inches away from the beach.
As we hit the sand, I jump over the side of the ship,
Soldiers and barbarians are flooding its side,
All screaming and yelling to cause fear.
Our archers are flinging arrows of fire into the huts.
The town bursts into flames.
I hope Thor was punishing them with a rain of fire
I can smell the burning flesh of the town's people.
The town burned to ash lay on the hillside
Not one living thing of value is left.
I silently walk through the town.
My men are still eager for attack,
But there's nothing left.
I look off through the fog and onto the ocean.
My fleet sits over the horizon
But only one ship is wedged into the sand,
Solitary and separated from the rest of the fleet.
It's my ship.
Silently my men climb into the ship
Everyone is thinking the same thing,
"Why were we left behind?"

A Day In the Life of a War
by Joseph Castaldi

On the battlefield ...
We were all waiting for the first shot to be fired.
I was engrossed in profound thought
thinking, "What was I actually doing out here?"
The loud bang of the first shot sent me back into reality.
The order was given to ready yourself,
and the directions given were very lucid.
Go out there, fight, and don't get yourselves killed.
This meant war.
Both of the sides charged into each other on the battleground,
trying to conserve energy
for when it was needed most.
When men started to get injured,
medics were disseminated to aid the wounded men,
So they could all be sent
Back on the battlefield ...

Philadelphia Flaws
by Brody Plourde

Every day I see crime.
It's everywhere and no matter how hard I try,
I cannot hide from it.
People do not contemplate what could happen, when they commit a crime,
They are too worried about the "getaway plan" and possible conviction.
They are so engrossed in killing or injuring other people.
They put pain into their victims and their families.
They get the chance to redeem themselves; however,
they seem to end up where they started,
in a cold place with orange clothes surrounded by bars.
I can see flaws in our so-called perfect world.
I see a world full of discrimination, hate, judgment, and killing.
It does not seem like "The City of Brotherly Love" sometimes.
People will see that nothing good comes from crime,
just deep pain,
just problems that can't be fixed by saying "sorry."

Snow
by Trudy Chung

I looked out, and see white flakes.
Falling, gently, to the ground.
I see children playing, laughing and having fun.
All covered in snow like sprinkles on ice cream.
I feel the air, so bitter and cold.
I smell the air and it burns my nose
I looked out and this time I see ...
... nothing.
Thousands of white flakes dotted the sky
I hear nothing
No one is outside

Cinderella
by Maura Rae Donapel

Ding dong! Ding dong!
Everything has gone wrong!
A glass slipper is missing,
The prince is harassing,
Ding dong! Ding dong!
Blink! Blink!
The slipper fell off within a wink.
Cinderella kept going
Without even knowing.
The prince was trying to think.

The Hallway
by Marlon Bayer

I enter the hallway–
A gateway to another world.
Walls are covered with deep cracks.
I start to move.
The weak wood creaks and cracks
step after step
Cobwebs cover the blank walls–
bare but for a lone painting.
It sits in the middle of the wall,
waiting for attention,
Waiting to be known,
Waiting,
Waiting.

When Life Gives You a Piano– Play It
by Charley Furtaw

As I sit down
I glance over my left shoulder
At the crowd
There is not much
Maybe 100 people
But it scares me
I turn back and look at my music
Get comfortable in my seat
Take one deep breath
Then two
Then three
And I play–
Play the piano
I can see my hands on the piano
Moving from key to key
I cannot think of anything else
No outside distractions
And I am done–
Done my song
I try to preserve it
By putting on the pedal for the last note
Everyone claps
I feel great
But as I walk
Down to my seat
Thoughts are racing through my mind
Did I do well?
I messed up–
Did I?
I don't think so
But then I stopped thinking
Only one thing comes to my mind
I don't care what anyone thinks
I did the best of my ability.

Stop, and Think
by Michael McKenna

Sometimes I stop and think
About the world around me
I think about wars and crimes
And how strange they all are
How people hurt each other,
for no apparent reason.
But then I think about this:
If everything was always fine and grand
We wouldn't appreciate their value
We would take them for granted.
Things can really be put in perspective
If one will just stop and think.

A Victim of Terrorism
by Richard Cavallaro

Every night I wake to the sounds of bombs
And every morning to the sounds of death.
There are no morals, laws, or kindness because of the lack of trust.
Families that helped me, children I played with,
Gone ... all because of religious segregation.
As I wake up to the rugged sand, I can only imagine.
American soldiers, coming to neutralize the threats of terrorism,
conserving our culture.
Even them we cannot trust; trust is dangerous here.
Many deaths have made lucid the penalties we face.
The struggles we face lead us further into darkness.
But why?
So we can compensate for other people's wrong doing?
As a young child, I wonder what the world is like.
Do people even contemplate my struggles, our struggles?
When I wake to death and despair, I wonder, who can help us?
Why is the world like this?
Please, I need to know, to see, and to feel a change in my life.

Dance
by Carly Hope

Dance
Fiery, Sassy
Jeté, Plié, Fouetté, Relevé
Swaying, Twirling, Whirling, Moving
Couru, Piqué, Tour, Balancé
Fun, Exciting
Art

The Tree
by Ashlynn Massimiano

Looking at the barren limbs on the tree,
I am wishing there is more to see.
Knowing that there is ample room for growth,
I'll be watching and waiting for this tree to surpass the rest ...
The time will come to see its extensive coverage.
The time will come to see its springtime blossoms.
In her glory, she will flourish with foliage.
Ultimately, she will blend in with the rest.

Aquilante Strong
by Vincent Corridoni

Every day is a struggle without you, Grandpa.
I'll never forget the memories we had together,
because you were the one who made them ...
Unforgettable!
I'll never find anyone who will be a role model for me
Like you ... kind, generous and funny.
I had no time to say goodbye ...
No time to wave at you.
You left
Before we knew it ...
Only God knows why.
No one will ever understand what it meant
To love you.
No one will ever know the power
Of Aquilante Strong!
I miss you Pop-Pop
I love you.

My Best Friend
by Ricquela McLeod

As I gaze into the vast, high plain of stars,
I laugh alongside the dancing fireflies.
The soft still river reflects his vibrant, white glow,
I know that as the world sleeps, he listens carefully to the night.
The day is very lonely because he is not there, but
I know I'll see him after his sister sets.
I scan the dusk sky and wait for return, and
At last I watch in wonder as he rises.
He is my best friend,
I love his lunar mist that fills my dreams.
The very sight of that beautiful, white, and
Floating orb in the sky turns my eyes into a hot waterfall.
I cannot resist the sheer beauty of the moon, and
The way he enters my thoughts while I sleep.
Others may see him, but he is mine only,
Because he is my best friend.

Upside Down Today
by Christina Paski

The bench that was once brown is now blue.
The sky that's up is now down.
A creature eats its lunch inside out.
The world seems to be upside down today.
People wear their shoes on their hands, and gloves on their feet.
The geniuses stop thinking, while the mousy ponder problems.
Trees bend while the flowers are stiff.
The world seems to be backwards today.
Giants cease to be a fantasy.
Gnomes come to life.
My feet become rubber.
The world becomes inside out.
Buildings shrink.
Bugs grow tall.
Birds dig instead of fly.
The world has seemed to have turned on its side.
I wish to know.
I wish to understand.
Why today seems so strange ...
More than usual.

Flowers
by Andrew Mason

Bundles of flowers bloom like freshly grown foods in a garden
Vibrant with color and glowing in the sun
The petals are one with the stem until they are separated by the wind
And settle into the grass as the breeze takes them away with a "whoosh"
They fly far away into a field filled with endless grass and green
They land very quietly without a "thud"
And brighten the field with so many different shades of color and they land
And become part of the pretty scene
The petals land and join together like they already know each other
And have a strong rapport
And when they join it is like a rainbow in a field
And this all happens
As old flowers die and new ones grow in

Spring
by Christopher Fagley

There it was–
The first signs of spring–
Just a signal
For when flowers start to bloom
and the snow goes away.
The grass turns green
and the sun starts to shine.
Animals prowl
and the church bells ring.
The cold turns to warmth.
Children, having fun,
pick flowers.
People, playing sports,
practice in the park
No wonder everyone loves spring.
It's the season of nature
and the time for spring cleaning
Watch– life is happening.

Love
by Peyton Nelson

Love is patient
Love is kind
Love is amazing
Love is blind
Love is putting someone before yourself
Love is not caring about what anyone else things
Love is the wind on a hot and sunny day
Love is the heat on a cold winter's night
Being in love is really a blast
It might feel like a rush
But don't forget to always remember
It's not love, it's lush.

Dreams
by Nadya Fam

In the first sweet sleep of night
The Nightingale tells a fairy tale
A magical dream of light
In a land where dreams set sail
Full of anger and hate, alone in the castle
An innocent walk leads Beauty to the Beast
The time runs out, with a rose in the vessel
Love broke the spell, let anger and hate cease
A change of fate, a dance under the silver light
The moon is bright, when the clock struck midnight
Magic, clock, and one lost shoe
All find their way to "I love you"
With a prick on the finger, Beauty sleeps in the tower
Guarded by the fiery beast, let a whole lifetime pass
The brave knight on a horse in shiny armor
Brings a kiss to her lips, ends the slumber at last
Once upon a time it's a happily ever after
It's a little girl's dream, full of joy and laughter
Like the sweet dreams of night, impossible as it seems
The fairy tale tells not to give up her dream

Rainy Days
by Rio The

Rainy days are gloomy
Rainy days are sad
Rainy days are miserable
The sun doesn't come out on a rainy day
The sun is hiding behind the dark clouds
The sun doesn't come out until the next sunny day
On a rainy day we can't go outside
A rainy day is a boring day because we can't go outside and play
A rainy day means no beach days and no swim days
Rainy days ruin plans
Rainy days ruin fun times outside
Rainy days are a good time to relax
Rainy days are a good time to watch movies

October
by Nyla Sanabria

October gave a party
The leaves by hundreds came
The chestnuts, oaks, and maples
And leaves of every name.
The sunshine glistened along the road
As I skipped with joy
And stepped upon the colorful autumn leaves.
I saw my friends and told them to come
To October's wonderful party
And told them it'll be fun.
As they follow
On the beautiful day
We set a bonfire for us to warm in the chilly weather.
Now October begins to sing a melancholy lullaby
With the colors of her voice in the deep wind
As beautiful as the sounds of a violin.
As we drift off in a nice peaceful sleep
We dream about the adventures
Of another autumn day.

A Burst of Anger
by Ian Kennedy

As rage destroys me from inside out, I feel nothing.
Rage is the only thing that matters.
The rage rushes through and takes control.
I unleash the rage and it destroys.
The rage starts dying and I begin to see what I've done.
I try to apologize, but it is too late.
I feels like the devil had me in his grasp.
Next time, I will defeat the dark side of anger.

Dreams
by Olivia Foxhill

Close your eyes and dream
Fly across the sky
Wish upon a star
Show who you really are
Release what was inside
Do what can't be done
Break the unbreakable
Think the unthinkable
Do the impossible
Dreams aren't unstoppable ...

The Power of Colors
by Alexandra DeTreux

For years the sun and rain were in a deadly battle.
During this time the people had no color.
Because of this, there were no emotions, and the Earth suffered.
Until one day the sun and rain noticed, the world was dying.
So they stopped their war.
After this happened, a great swarm of color united over the land.
It was restored!
The people could love, and feel happiness once more.
All because,
The colors of a RAINBOW.

Frontline
by Colby Alvarado

Soldiers are running
As guns are humming
Thousands of feet
Running through the streets
Planes are soaring
As the engines are roaring
Tanks roll through the streets
Heavy enough to destroy the concrete
The streets are filled with light
As the soldiers fight
Soldiers run through gunfire
As soldiers tire
Soldiers throw grenades
And the enemies run away
Blood is shed
As others continue ahead

Racing
by Tessa Bewley

It was the middle of summer
Which wasn't such a bummer
There was a man who was pacing
Because he was getting ready for some racing
The man climbs into his car
As he pulls his belts tight
He gets pushed off to start the engine
As the other drivers get ready to fight
They line up to take the green
As they go roaring into the turn
All the cars were clean
But, the one car crashes and burns
He got out of the car
He is okay
He will race another day
So, he and his crew will have to drive far

Free
by Kate Hafer

I feel free, oh so free!
Like a bird in a bright blue sky,
soaring elegantly around the sun.
I feel free, oh so free!
Like a monarch butterfly in a field of flowers,
sipping nectar one flower at a time.
I feel free, oh so free!

Last Summer Sunset
by Bridget Benson

The river's meandering crystal clear halcyon waters,
until the rapids pin water onto the mammoth boulders,
the mountain's rugged edge, sharp as shark teeth,
the depth of the valley covered in wildflowers,
with the river dancing through its median,
behind the valley is the mountains, reaching up to touch the clouds,
altogether the lustrous river, the razor-sharp mountains,
and the valley dotted with brilliant colors,
watch the last summer sunset,
beautiful, dazzling, as if untouched by humans.

Brown
by Nastasha Parkkila

Brown is a fence,
guarding the garden.
Brown is the soil,
in the ground and under the grass.
Brown is a graham cracker,
better smelling than dirt.
Brown is a monkey,
jumping from tree to tree.
Brown is fur,
softer than a baby's skin.
Brown is wood,
rough and bumpy.
Brown is chocolate,
tastier than marshmallows.

She Is Gone
by Piper Myers-Poppay

She is there, eyes flutter as she lies unconscious.
Her hair falls in neat curls on her head, like smoke from a pipe.
The doctor removes her oxygen cannula from her nose.
She gasps and heaves till her lips turn frosty blue like a frozen lake.
I sit then by her side, a single tear swivels down my face,
I wipe it away with my sleeve.
Her once rosy cheeks turned icy white.
Oh God, I moan, I don't think I can handle this.
My tears are raining down now.
She is gone
A hole of grief burns in my stomach and I feel like I am going to throw up.
She is gone and there is nothing I can do about it
She is gone, her eyes wide, staring at nothing at all
She is gone

Is It Just a Dream?
by Mekenzie Hancock

I watched the steam as we drove away
fog up the window, I didn't have a say
The cold from outside, chilled me to the bone
the Illinois winters, I used to call home.
Where we headed I could only imagine
this place we were going I just couldn't fathom.
I heard it's called Idaho I think
might as well be China, I felt my heart sink.
A foreign land ahead, didn't know what to expect
I just knew I felt alone, alone in my head ...
Mountains, rivers, blue skies above ...
was it Heaven or did I just fall in love?
This new place I call home, was it better than before?
New family, new friends! How could I ask for more!
I pause for a moment, turn my face to the sky.
My heart leaps inside me, and I think I know why ...
Thank you Mom, you only wanted the best,
you never gave up, never settled for less!
Thanks for the faith it's helped guide my way.
I look to it for strength each and every day.

Untitled
by Daniel Kristoff

Her hair flows in the wind as if it was water off a cliff.
Her eyes twinkle as if they were carved out of stars.
Her personality flies like a bird flies through the air.
The way she smiles is almost magical.
It makes your mind wonder if you are in a magical dream world.
Making you question everything else in the world.
But you have to believe at some point.

When Night Comes
by Lauren Blick

When the light is shining bright, I have no fear
But when they go out and I'm left in darkness
Is when I grow drear
The shadows linger throughout
The darkness roaming about
Yet when I turn on the light
They seem to disappear
This mystery seems unclear
Why they roam in the dark, and leave in the light
I know when I go to sleep, they will be here tonight

Spring Breeze
by Hannah Ward

Trees and flowers are blooming
such a great sight to see
come along and see with me.
There are roses, violets too
aren't they a beautiful sight to see.
Birds are chirping
bees are buzzing
And fireflies are glowing
And just a light spring breeze is blowing.
The sun is hot but the pool is not
So go jump in and race your friends
show them what you got.
Don't stay inside all day
Go out and play
on this beautiful spring day.

Today
by Quadree Kenner

Today is the day
This is the one
Today is the day
Today we'll be kind
Today is important
So don't you leave it behind
Let's do it all and never stop
No matter what's on the clock
You better have fun because after all it
Will just POP!!!

My Candyrific Dream
by Jeneyan Marley

One night I had a wonderful dream.
It was filled with candy and ice cream.
I ate all I could and all I could carry.
Till my mom woke me up and my dream was over in a hurry.
But I'll still remember the ice cream man that sat in a corner.
Though now the dream is hard to remember.
Once in a while I try to go back.
To see all my candy friends all over again.

Dance
by Amber Forehand

Teachers teacher
Hard-working
Always learning something new
Music playing
Hours practicing
But it's always fun to do
Hundreds of turns and jumps
Never perfect
Many tries
And sometimes gets blisters and bumps
But soon enough there is a recital
And it's all worth it and is a lot of fun.

Nature
by Joey Hubmaster

Nature is wonderful.
All the shapes and sizes of clouds and trees,
and there are still a lot more things.
All the vibrant colors and animals and insects.
Buzzing and running around,
the beautiful,
wonderful world.

All About Me
by Icheir Thorn

I love sports. I love seafood. I want everything.
I'm sporty. I love my family. My favorite color is sky blue.
I love the Xbox One, PS4, and I want more.
I have 4 brothers and 1 sister.
My favorite basketball player is LeBron James.
I want to be a football or basketball player.
My friend wants to be a mayor.
I'd love friend chicken but I like salmon.
I love my mom. I want to be rich.
I don't want to be like Mitch from Regular Show
or Moon from Grand Theft Auto.

Pamaj
by Stephen Cianci

Pamaj is a famous COD gamer
I watch his YouTube channel
He's as skilled as a painter
He'll have a COD battle
He's got 1 million subs that are loyal
While he never misses a shot
When he kills people their heads start to boil
Some would cheat by using aimbot
Pamaj will live on
Legacy and name
People will watch him on their lawn
For Pamaj is far from lame
There's no way to tell how much he won
And yet he will rarely ever lose
You're always sad when his videos are done
How great it would be to live in his shoes

Daddy's Little Girl
by Calai'f Nelson

Dad, I know you go through a lot of pain
That you don't even have time to maintain
I know you went through an aneurysm and stroke
And I want you to know that broke my heart
I know I'm Daddy's little girl
And I know that you loved the way I used to twirl
And you're the best dad in the whole wide world
And I hope you know that I love, I will look above
You
Happiness, I can't live without you
People laugh at me
Because they have no honesty
And when I think of you, Dad
It makes me really sad

Pretty Doesn't Hurt
by Adrianna Fields

I feel the power to be pretty,
Be myself,
And rock on!
You don't need makeup,
You don't need lipstick,
You don't need plastic surgery,
And you don't need advice.
Us young ladies are perfect the way we are.
You can wear what you want,
You can be who you want,
Just don't try to be pretty
Beyoncé may be right about it hurting
But don't be pretty
Be beautiful

Family
by Jannessa Rogers

People drive me crazy
Even the people I call family
My family is insane
My sister has no brain
And she has an attitude
My dad likes to go mudding and hunting
My mom likes to stay home

Jesus Gift
by Christina Zogar

The greatest present that
Jesus had ever given long
Ago wasn't wrapped up in
A box or tied with a bow.
God's only Son from Heaven
Above given straight
From His heart. The greatest
Gift brought on that night.
His gift of love for all
Eternity and his gift of happiness for
Those who believe. From
That night to the light
Jesus is watching us all day
Long.

Dreams Are Real
by Aaliyah Mickens

My dreams are real, I see them everywhere.
I've got good creatures and bad creatures all around.
Am I nuts or crazy because a goose tried to date me.
Every night before I go to sleep,
I pray to God my soul to keep,
But then a ghost goes through me and takes my soul
Now it's dark and cold.
To make these monsters go away
I think and then a portal comes,
That's when I make my way through the portal, then bam!
I wake up, another night goes by, but the same dream I have,
Is it a nightmare or a curse, I don't know!

The Impossible Man
by Jordan Scott

A man who was there for it all,
He witnessed the Romans' rise and fall,
He heard President Reagan speak the words,
"Mr. Gorbachev, tear down this wall."
He has taken us back, we have fallen and began to crawl.
He has witnessed us fall time and time again,
and picked us up with a simple amen.
He gave us eternal life by losing his own
He paid for our sins by the pain of the cross and stone
This man is God
and He has saved the flawed.
He has saved us from death,
By giving us His Son's last breath

Walking, Walking, and More Walking
by Allison Henwood

It's pouring and storming, and my socks are all wet.
I have to walk my entire street, and I'm not even walking a pet.
My dad won't pick me up, and I'm exhausted from school.
Rain is dripping from my clothes. I feel like I'm in a swimming pool.
Dad please come get me, and wake from your dream.
I'm getting even more wet. Now the street is pretty much just a stream.
I also have to walk my driveway, and that's about a mile.
I'm a very slow walker. It will take me a while.
I'm almost there, at the very top.
My driveway's a mountain. I cannot stop.
I'm now at my house, and I open the door.
I see my dad on the couch, and he makes a really loud snore.
I go back to my room, and I change my clothes.
I put on dry socks, so I can warm my toes.
I'm now warm and dry, and to my sister I say,
"I know our dad works a lot, but do we really have to walk every day?"

My Chicken Pot Pie
by Dane Klahold

There was a small pickle
who found himself a nickel
he gave it to a homeless guy
he said he wanted some chicken pot pie.
He went to the grocery store
so he could find some more
they were sold out
so he gave out a loud shout.
He went to his mom's house
where he had a pet mouse
he found some on the stove
he heated for the go.
He ran to the homeless guy
to give him the chicken pot pie
he smiled with delight
after that I never seen his sight.

Death
by Justin Forbes

I feel Death's cold and stony grasp brush up against my shoulders,
it feels like I am in a cold and dark freezer, but there is nothing in there but me.
I push it away and run in the opposite direction,
I will see my family, my coma will not kill me,
I try to find a way to wake up and see my family, yet it seems I may die.
The blanket of darkness seems to have caught up with me, yet again.
I try to will myself to wake up, but still find myself trying to escape death,
this time I try a new direction and go away from the darkness.
I run for what seems like hours, and still the darkness shows no signs of relenting.
I try and go on but it seems I have no strength,
then my family and friends come to mind and I think of them,
with them in my head I push on no matter what pain I feel.
It seems that I see a small light in the distance in all the darkness
I know what it is it, it is my way out
I sprint trying to beat the darkness
but it's almost like I can feel its breath right on my back,
I have a few paces when the darkness surrounds me.
I lost, I know this is the end of my fight,
I close my eyes and I embrace death.
I feel no pain but I know I have died,
I open my eyes, I am in Heaven with God.

Drama
by Jenna Johnson

When you turn your back, everyone betrays you
Your friend is a black hole in the universe
You think they're your friend then BAM they're gone
They make you swell up in a pool of sorrow.
Some friends make you lose your relationship with others
They make you feel like they're invisible, non-existing
You make me blow into a million pieces
You feel like you will never be put together again
It crushes you

A Wild Ride
by Kolby West

My uncle had a pony that needed stuck.
He bragged that this gelding could really buck.
I thought he was just being silly.
That horse seemed calm as a filly.
Full grown he barely passed my uncle's knee,
so I knew he couldn't be tougher than me.
I got real bored and rode him outta the cage,
by the way he bucked I could feel his rage.
I was trying to ride that critter out
But he just kept bucking about.
Before ya know it, I'm sittin' in the dirt
I climb back on, but I'm starting to feel the hurt
He ran speedily across the street,
And it was clear he couldn't be beat.
He sped to some other horses,
It was true they had strong forces.
He tried getting in their fence.
The power was much too immense.
I rode that rough-neck back,
My strength at a big lack.
After I got off that mean old jerk,
I looked in his eyes and saw a smirk.
Walking to the house I felt like a hack
This lil' cowpoke needed to hit the sack
So next time you under estimate a horse that's small
Remember even a pony can make a man like me fall.

Home On Thanksgiving
by James McCarthy

I can smell turkey cooking in the oven.
I can hear gravy boiling on the stove.
I can taste Mom's pumpkin pie.
I love being home on Thanksgiving.
My family just knocked on the door.
I'll eat all I can.
We'll play cards all night long.
I love being home on Thanksgiving.

Family
by Rylee Hutchinson

I'm from popcorn and a movie every Friday night.
From big brown eyes and dark thick hair.
I'm from Mom and Dad, Bubba and Josie, Gwen and Amanda.
From playing video games until you reach the next level.
I'm from eating different foods every night, never the same thing.
I'm from running into my sister's room every time I hear a sound.
From turning up the volume every time Mom wants me to do something.
From running around outside on the rocks with bare feet.
I'm from saying the pledge every day at school.
From loving my English class and writing lots of poems.

She's Unknown
by Adrianna Roy

This girl sits in the back of the class,
Always getting picked last
She has thoughts of skipping it, 'cause she thought, "Who'd notice?"
She's so caught up with the mean words so she can't focus
Failing every test, not ever can she be the best,
See, 'cause she can't be enough, no one knows her life is tough
When she goes to bed she has the horrible thoughts in her head
Her dad died and it makes her really sad
Mom leaves her and she doesn't know why, that's why she breaks down and cry
Every night she paints a picture but it ain't on any paper
It's on her arms and legs, and soon as she's done she wants to take a break
She's in a conflict, she's so sick and tired of being punched and kicked
She gets ready for the day, she wears a mask so no one would ask if she's okay
No one knows who she is, 'cause no one knows who unknown is …

Why Not
by Taniyah Mason

Why me?? Curious as anyone
can ever be. Why me?? I
really want to know so let me see.
Let me see the answer to my
question. You could have chosen her,
him, she, he, but why pick me?
Never mind my question because
It's not being answered. I'll just
be myself and take this challenge.
Why Shouldn't I?? Why not?

Lion Heart
by Kennedy Howell

My heart is like a lion's
Fierce but kind
I am the protector of the group
Even though I am small
If you make me mad you better get out of my way
Or you will regret your decision
Even though I am quiet, I am loud
I will help you up if you fall down
I may have the heart of a lion, but I have some characteristics too

Joe's Story
by Jaden Tilley

Joe was amazing
He was awesome
Joe could run faster than a sloth
He could swim better than a cat
He was smarter than a chicken
That is funny because that's his nickname
He could walk better than a bird
He could fly better than a penguin
Joe was the most popular person at his school
But Joe had a secret
He had a broken heart
His pet caterpillar disappeared
When that butterfly showed up

Divorce: Weathering the Storm
by Chloe Schlack

Divorce,
It isn't a flower bed.
It is a rosebush, thorns and all.
It is an eternal dark cloud over your rainbow.
Changes start racing to the finish line.
Your life begins to fall like the leaves on a tree.
A thunderstorm right before your eyes.
A hurricane between you and your family.
A tornado in your bond.
A tsunami throughout your childhood.
An earthquake in your life.
But at the end of this will be a rainbow.
She will take care of you.
For she is Hope.
Her arms wrap around you to dry your tears.
She keeps you safe and sound.

Roses Will Regrow
by Alice Ivashina

When roses die we learn
That one day we'll be gone
Our petals perish through the years
And we realize our biggest fears
Of pain and suffering and death
Of when we take our final breath
We concentrate too much on fate
So don't just sit around and wait
Feel happy when you say goodbye
For that's the greatest way to die
So when the roses get so old
That life brings them an end
Don't try to make it stop or slow
New roses will regrow

The Rush
by Tara Shores

Snap! I'm hooked in.
There is no escaping the rush of excitement.
The snow glistens in the sunlight, goggles are pulled down into place,
and poles are in hands.
The mountain is calling, and I must respond.
My breath is visible in the air.
I bend, preparing myself for the cool rush of air
about to hit my face like a sudden slap.
Prepared, I drop in, feeling the snow scrape the bottoms of my skis
as I glide down the mountain.
Snowboarders, skiers, silky snow.
All of our shadows projecting on the snow
as we prepare ourselves to sit on the lift once again.

I Love To Dance
by Isabel Taylor

Jazzing it up with Skater Boy
a floating moonbeam in ballet
flapped my wings in Swan Lake
at the magical lake
chasing butterflies in Wonderland
but my favorite has to be Nutcracker
the party was fun
we laughed and danced, the soldier doll arrived
the snowflakes came down
when we entered the land of the sweets
also we sipped Chinese tea
as we ate Marzipan treats
I danced in Circus
a newsboy protesting
newspaper prices
waiting till the love runs out
was blown away by Carrie Underwood
a Serenade
and a Cupid
Oh, I love to dance

My Day
by Megan Iannacone

My dog sat there waiting for me to wake up,
He was crying as loud as a pup,
When I did awake I was as happy as I could be,
My dog was so happy to see me,
I picked him up and went downstairs,
I said my morning prayers,
I said good morning to my mom and dad,
Then my dog started to get sad,
Of course! I have to take him for a walk,
As I was walking down the block,
Boom, my neighbor was right there,
As if I didn't know where,
I said hello,
But I had to go
That's my day,
Now off to play.

Flying By
by Alexander Borda

Getting ready for the race,
Lacing up my bright shoes and my black brace,
Getting ready for the race,
Gathering up my teammates.
I hit the rocky dirt,
With a kick start,
Feeling the warm air on my skin,
As I glide like a cloud across the bright blue sky.
The sound of my shoes hitting the road,
Gets me in my rhythm and my mode,
I start to get ahead of the pack,
And start to near the end of the track.
The pressure mounts,
This last kick counts,
Flying by,
Flying by.

My Homework Does Not Love ME
by Olivia Amorando

Homework oh homework
Oh how I love my homework,
But my homework does not love me
Although I try and try again
I cannot succeed
Math and science and social studies oh my
My head is swirling with 2+2=Abraham Lincoln
But why do I not succeed
Maybe it's the world around me singing their songs of joy
Though I cannot seem to get it right

The Music That Flows Through My Hands
by Sarah Abdalla

I feel an odd sensation,
That is crawling up my arm.
It starts out small and queer,
Before turning into an alarm.
As I rush to the keys,
And quickly snatch my book.
I plop down on my seat,
And open it up to look.
Paging through its contents,
I find songs from A-Z.
But I choose a particular piece,
By the famous Tchaikovsky.
Finally, I let loose.
All of my stress is gone,
Into a new, improved way of feeling,
Oh, let the music go on and on.
Above the keys I hold my fingers,
Hovering in suspense.
Until I play the grand finale,
Now, all my time is spent.

Stinky, Slimy Socks
by Hannah Rogers

Stinky, slimy socks
So icky, blicky gross
Sitting in my room
Smelling like old toast
Stinky, slimy socks
So icky, blicky gross
Sitting in the bathroom
Smelling like moldy crab
Stinky, slimy socks
So icky, blicky gross
Sitting in the living room
Smelling like gym sweat
Stinky, slimy socks
So icky, blicky gross
Sitting in the laundry room
Smelling like pumpkin spice

Why
by Emmaline Hubbs

Why is life so fragile–
Why is time so rushed
Why is a soul forever;
Why is a whisper hushed
Why is the sky freedom;
Why is the ocean blue
Why are the stars hope–
Why in dreams do we pursue
Why draw unseen boundaries–
Why put the daring down
Why keep prominent voices quiet;
Why limit one's ability to grow profound
Why is life so fragile
Why is time so rushed
Why is a soul forever
Why is a whisper hushed
Questions are our savior
Knowledge is our prize
Answers are our dreams
But curiosity forever lingers in our eyes

Dreams
by Niko Bianco

Lacing up my shoes.
Stepping onto that wood court.
Having dreams come true.

The Vicious Lies
by Damian Glenn

Part of me is independent yellow.
Dedicated and exhilarated.
Sympathetic and confident.
Proudly carrying the weight of others.
But deep inside, there is another part,
Misunderstood velvet, like a wounded dog, who doesn't obey.
Neglected and abandoned,
Confused and unwanted,
Unable to control the vicious lies.
Both of these sides of me are very real,
Seeking out someone to trust with my pain

Too Cool For School
by Sam Transtrum

I just woke up, I'm late for school.
I don't want to go, I'm low on fuel.
It's only Tuesday, I'm already bored,
If it were the weekend, I'd party galore.
I don't want to get ready, I won't comb my hair.
My mom will soon make me, but I really don't care.
Yet here I am, sitting, so tired I might drool,
Yep, life's really tough when you're too cool for school.
I've tried to be active, I've done quite a bit.
It didn't work out well, I had quite a fit.
I finally got dressed, though it took lots of fuss,
I'm walking to school 'cause I missed the bus.
Then I started to think, walking through the bike lane,
If you can't change it, then why complain?
And if I am wrong, please don't call me a fool,
But I don't think anyone's too cool for school.

Memorable Mistakes
by April Chronowski

Life is short, so make it count.
Don't do everything perfect.
If everything is right, what will we remember?
How will we laugh at the bloopers of our lives?
If there are none?
So make mistakes.
Our mistakes are our memories.

Remembering Happiness
by Elizabeth Miller

You may sit,
And calmly wait,
To watch the wind blow,
But all you can imagine is,
The dark nightmares you had,
Not even a single dream,
You can see,
In the distance,
Sun's rays,
Seeping through the clouds,
And you finally remember,
The happiness,
That once was in your life ...

Superheroes
by Sameer Sharma

Superman is strong and tall,
But Batman owns a mall.
The Flash is very fast,
But The Reverse can go back to the past.
Thor has the power of lightning,
And The Hulk is very frightening.
Captain America is the winter soldier,
But Iron Man can destroy a bunch of boulders.
Wonder Woman has many powers,
But Black Widow owns many towers.
Star-Fire is from a different planet,
And Raven is always in a panic.

Things That Stink
by Charlie Ford

My little cousin and my dog,
My big cousin and a dead frog,
Occasionally the neighborhood skunk,
And the spilled milk in my mom's trunk,
James and his dirty socks,
and my cat's litter box,
There are many things that stink
and sometimes me.

A Court Haven
by Calista Hall

Part of me is burnt orange.
Fired up and energetic,
Confident and considerate,
Fighting for the ball and team win.
But deep inside, there is another part,
Dark grey, like a fluttering, fleeing bird.
Anxious and overwhelmed,
Confused and impatient,
Thinking of being on the court where I can be me.
Both of these sides are very real,
Sometimes feeling like a soaked tree with its head down,
yet bright and cheerful most of the time.

On the Horizon
by Connor Barclay

On the horizon the enemies approach,
as he wields his sword for battle,
he saddles his horse and starts to ride off,
the enemies ready their bows,
arrows are fired through the crimson sky,
he stops and doesn't retaliate,
the sky goes from crimson to midnight black,
as a shower of arrows passes over,
he pulls out his shield and feels,
the vibration of arrowheads piercing the shield,
he then turns back and accepts what is his defeat.

Unplugging
by Martin Anders Whipple

You swipe your hand or press the light,
bracing for the incoming delight.
The room lights up in a fury of lights,
stretching throughout the night.
You hear movement on the streets,
most likely people going home to sleep.
You look at the time,
it is later than you'd like, but you don't mind.
You're stuck, bound by your own conscience.
Do you think of those lights as a treat or an addiction?

Black Marsh
by Lauren Hagen

In the land
Lies a marsh
It's a place
Much more than harsh
Beyond the trees
Above the soil
Lies an evil
Ready to uncoil
No sounds are made
In a state of silence
They've forgotten
Its past of violence
Far past the leaves
What lies there for years
A darkness like no other
Beyond all fears
If the darkness comes upon you
There is no going back
And there is no forgiveness
Of the marsh shadowed black

The Dream
by Sophia Gabelberger

Come you lords, come you ladies, join the midnight dance.
Throw angry beauties and graceful pains, into the bag of chance.
Come whether fireflies or snowflakes dot the sky
Come lords, come ladies, come, and remember how to fly.
Come you children, come you babies, sit at the feet of a star
As they tell you a tale of wonder and places afar.
Whimsical and strange, never quite the same,
The night makes up the rules to his game,
The Earth is spinning the thread of who you are
When the wind arises, with a whistling song,
And the lords and ladies dance into the dawn,
They leave you with nothing, nothing to keep,
Nothing at all but a dream.

The Missing Magic
by Andrew Newman

I try to remember, with much despair
the magic, the bliss, the happiness
But it is broken beyond repair
no matter how much I hate this.
There was a time when all of the troubles
were but a distant dream,
but now it is real and it boils and bubbles
without peace as it used to seem.
However much I miss the past
I know it's been left behind
and all those things, I see at last,
that I had, was I out of my mind?!
to overlook the fortune I had,
how could I be so blind?
but now I see those things I had
had magic I didn't find.
I now continue life beyond
and make the world anew,
improve for those in time beyond
to have this magic, like me and you.

The World
by Isaiah Horlacher

The world is a scary, violent place
There is hunger, debt, and fear
It seems like everyone wants their own master race
People live in scary places and cry many tears
Authorities try to cover it up
But the truth is right here
We need to know what's going on
To be prepared to go out there
So I'll just keep on living
Just trying to prepare
For when I do go out there
I won't get caught in its snare

The Hungry People
by Paige Byerly

People at the border of the road and sidewalk,
fading away like dinosaurs once did.
Begging for money, diseased and weary.
They are craving a plentiful meal.
Fading away like dinosaurs once did.
The occasional coin plinks in their donation can.
They are craving a plentiful meal.
One wee grain of rice may be all they acquire.
The occasional coin plinks in their donation can.
Their stomachs praying for a better life.
One wee grain of rice may be all they acquire.
They are deserts, lacking food and drink.
Their stomachs praying for a better life.
People at the border of the road and sidewalk.
They are deserts, lacking food and drink,
begging for money, diseased and weary.

Sweet Childhood
by Max Lind

How good it is to be a guilt-free youth
Naive of all things bad and good alike
Who in his world knows not of in-between
But lives instead at one of the extremes
Who is afraid of monsters in the night
And loves to play a game of Peek-A-Boo
Who not yet knows the worth of those few years
Which are without a doubt the most divine
But gone is that good spell that lives so full
And lets the mind be filled with limitless content
For time has come to face reality
And learn to live in the hard knocks of life

Seasons
by Brendon Arcara

As green turns to yellow, and yellow turns to red,
this is a symbol that summer's almost dead.
Birds are flying to the south, and temperatures are getting low.
You can feel the seasons changing, as the winds begin to blow.
It's getting colder day and night; the cold is quite a pain.
There's no more green left in sight, as fall has started to strain.
No more birds are singing, for their nests are on the ground.
No more kids are swinging, for autumn's done its round.
Snow begins to pile up, gently falling from the clouds.
Not a piece of grass in sight, as winter takes the crown.
We realize we can actually go out and run after we fight a snowball fight.
Just when we thought school was done, winter decides to leave that night.
The sun is coming out to play, destroying all the snow.
Everybody is ecstatic today as Punxsutawney lets us know ...
Spring is here early. It's time to celebrate!
Just in time to recognize that winter's not that great!
Winter, spring, summer, and fall– which is the greatest of them all?
Now this question might not sound rather new,
but the best is the choice that is left up to you.

Left Behind
by Samantha Boutte

I knew it was too good to be true,
You flashed in and out of my life in a blink of an eye,
With nothing but me left behind,
No word of explanation,
No care in the world,
But look what you left,
A broken heart and no one to lean on,
She says she's ok but look deep inside her,
She needs to know she is needed and not forgotten,
But you are too conceited to see what you left behind.

Dreams
by Aubrie Calder

To dream is to be in a lively state,
it is where the mind creates.
Dreams come from what you say and do,
it creates a reflection of the inner you.
Daydreams choose where they want to go,
dreaming in peace has its own flow.
Nightmares go a scary way,
think good thoughts and they'll go away.
Some dreams you don't want to wake,
but you will and realize it's fake.
People think dreams stay inside,
instead some dreams make you burst with pride.
Let you and your dreams take flight,
it doesn't end when you sleep tonight.
No one can forever change the true dream,
let you and your imagination take it to the extreme.
Follow your dreams all the way through,
and you will realize they were following you.

Fate
by Alexander Green

The day we all believe
That our fate set in stone,
That we shall follow a distinct, unchangeable path,
Is the day we change it.
But the day we believe we are each independent
That we shall follow no one direct path
Is the day we seal it.

Nightmares
by William Jaskot

Nightmares are something of wonders.
A world of fear and pain like a labyrinth with no end.
Facing fears that haunt the back of your mind only to come out at night.
They run up and down your dreams chasing your mind
into an abyss of darkness.
Confronting trials trying to escape, but when you get to the end,
the nightmares trick you to go to the beginning of a new horror to face.
The nightmares consume all happiness, joy and light you can think of.
Like beasts with no soul, and dead eyes looking of a way
to destroy your courage.
But when the light comes through the window at the crack of dawn,
the darkness runs from the bright light speeding from corner to corner.
Not every bad dream makes it to the shadows.
The sun is a wall that the nightmares can't break.
When the nightmares run with the dark,
spreading from one end of the Earth to the other.
Terrorizing children and adults.
Waking them up with the fear to close their eyes again.
Little girls scared of big bugs crawling all around them.
But nightmares happen to teens too.
Teenage girls scared of a boy band losing one of their members
or teenage boys scared of some zombie apocalypse happening
and they can't get away from the swarms of zombies.
The nightmares take all the great parts of a day and mold it into a ball of pain
to be thrown right at the face.
The nightmares turn things into a fist to hit you in the gut,
knocking the wind out of you.
Nightmares are strong and clever things recreating anything to frighten us.
Truly, an unstoppable force.

Nothing Impossible
by Samantha Eill

Could be's and might be's may be
Real. Life, a blank canvas,
Waiting for an artist to create a
Masterpiece. Anything is
Possible. People are
Good. Nothing stands in your
Way. Monsters hide under the bed,
Princesses are trapped in a tower,
Childhood means
Hope,
Wonder, and that all
Fantasies are true, because
There is nothing
Impossible

In and Out
by Abagail Docimo-Ziccardi

You are a vast blue blanket that wraps around me
Breathing in and out
Rolling your hands gently across the shore
It ever so calms me
The moon whose light reflects on the dark night changes you ever so
Slowly you make your way up to kiss the shore with your cool lips
Breathing in and out
You are so kind to give your home to many
As you breathe many come and go through this world
Ripples and wrinkles are a part of your beauty
Even more when the storms roll in
There is no taming you
You calm just as you rage
Breathing in and out
Swirls of color and emotion
The sky reflects you
Oh how wonderful you can be
Breathing in and out
You are the ocean

America
by Ian Kendall

Sometimes I wonder
What's out there in yonder
Could it be guns and war?
or simply rocky shores?
Death and despair
by both land and air
all these things
on wheels and wings
will cause us all
a worldwide brawl
and if survival means
protecting ourselves with junky machines
then what does peace mean?

Gentle Wolves
by Aubrey Sauerwald

Little flowers swaying in the breeze
Birds singing in the trees
Her little red cloak carefree and naive
Mom said be careful when you leave.
Crunching of leaves next to me
That over there, what could it be
Thoughts in my head racing around
Hand on my neck I fall to the ground.
I didn't mean to startle you
May I ask, who are you?
Here take my hand I'll lead you through.
Should I trust him, what should I do?
Distracted by those crystal eyes
But, is it all just a dashing disguise.
As you are pretty so be smart,
Wolves may lurk in every part.
Beware the path because you may fall.
Gentle wolves are the most dangerous of all.

Water Crashing Onto the Surface
by Braden Brasch

This fall is very lacking
from what it may have been long ago.
A mighty, rushing, waterfall,
to a tiny stream with little flow
beside it are some pines,
so numerous in the fall.
All of which are healthy, strong,
and proudly standing tall.

Good Days
by Dani Kehs

There are some good days that come and pass sometimes
Those days just swing around me left and right
I'll probably go run and hide from my fear
Someday my life might disappear from me
What will I do ... I am all alone
I thought that my future would break my bones
Why go away good days?
Did you ever know that my fears weren't washed away?
My hope and joyfulness ran from me
Does this have to be my history?
My bad days have gone, my good days have come
Now I will make better everything that I've done

Words
by Daniel Will

Writing. So easy, so comforting, but hard.
Words still have to flow like the current of a stream.
They are simple and compound, short but sophisticated,
but all will make you think deeper into your language.
Your understanding of words will flourish.
You will develop new and effective skills to intrigue your reader,
like chocolate attracts children.
You really need to bring out the true feelings
of your reader towards your characters.
Make them glue their eyes to the sandy brown pages of your novel.
When you truly compose a bestseller, it will be read for centuries to come.

Dreams
by Matthew Dumagco

Frozen in time
memories don't see the light
dreams are the escape

World of Mystery
by Kaelah Baxter

I open a world of mystery, curious of what's on the pages.
I read about the characters and problems that occur.
Sadly, I read about the struggles.
Curious thoughts whir in my head.
I wonder about the things happening.
But then as I read more, I happily come to find that things are better!
The characters are saved, the problems overcome!
I close the back cover as the whirring, excited thoughts come to a standstill
And then I return the world of mystery that was given to me.
I search for an exciting adventure, pressured by my excitement to read.
As time is running out, I quickly grab one and take it home.
And with a blank, excited mind, eager to go on an adventure,
I open a world of mystery!

My Dear Beloved
by Ross Neuman

My love for you is like lovely fairies.
I'm not able to take my eyes off you.
Let me please have the allowance to marry.
There is nothing I would rather do.
If not, I will go and weep silently.
Oh yes my dear, then love will take my eye.
If no, my dream distraught so violently.
Then I will await wedding day with thy.
You have made me the man I want to be.
Please don't regret the decision you make.
The reason I cannot take my eyes off thee.
Our wedding day would taste like chocolate cake.
So if you decide to marry me.
I will become the happiest can be.

The John Totten Park
by Rhianna Gonzales

The building stands out,
Against the green and browns of the building.
The light pink of the blossoming cherry tree,
Makes the tan of the bricks look fake.
If you are facing just the right way,
you can't even see the football and baseball fields.
The laughter from the preschool playground,
Is the most beautiful part of the park.
Even though the lawnmower is mowing right next to us,
You can still hear the faint sound of birds chirping.
The way that we are fenced in like an insane asylum
Gives the park a cozy feeling.
The fact that the path hasn't been weeded in fifty years,
Gives the illusion that it's a blanket of green.
But nothing can compare to the scattered mulch,
At the base of the pine tree.

A Girl's Best Friend
by Jacqueline Swartz

When I look at his face my soul lights up
His big brown eyes and golden coat of fur
Gentle, calm, and majestic, he is so
Even his bark, so wondrous it is
The smell of grass and dirt rubs off on him
I feel his soft fur coat, it's like a cloud
The flawless way which he carries himself
I hear his dog tag jingle as he moves
His tail wags, his fur blows, as he prances
Sit, stay, paw, come, commands he will obey
So strong, so brave, the way he frolics forth
Yet oh so calm, and quiet I would say
He's always aware when problems occur
Perfect though, a true perfect girl's best friend

Mrs. Felter
by James Steffy

Mrs. Felter
Mrs. Felter
Mrs. Felter
Happy Mrs. Felter
Love Mrs. Felter
Good, fun, joy Mrs. Felter
Funny, excitement, enjoys Mrs. Felter
Those are just a few
Kind Mrs. Felter
Self-control Mrs. Felter
Exciting, running, jumping Mrs. Felter
Juggling, bundling, snuggling Mrs. Felter
Nice Mrs. Felter too
Patient Mrs. Felter
Faithful Mrs. Felter
Don't forget peace Mrs. Felter
Last of all– best of all– I like fun Mrs. Felter

Ode To Cup
by Lucas Lia

Made in China, but relocated here,
Your sturdy features and perfect physique
Can compare to no other cup.
The reflected light dances with the foreground;
I love thee, but alas, thee loves New York!
The optimal form for grip
Holds liquids easily without fail.
A dazzling white with brooding red
Holding all up to eight large ounces.
Impervious to all damage, less revealing only cracks,
Can withstand all, hot or cold.
Dexterous and flexible,
Composed of only the finest porcelain fragments.
A solid three-inch diameter,
Thick rimmed, a bold message.
So royal, copy written by only the great Kings™
Dented from years of wear and worn,
Hidden with a secret barcode message,
You are both hollow, yet brimming with life.

Ralph, Ronald, Rover, Rold
by Laura Feeney

Ralph Ronald Rover Rold
Always felt extremely cold
His home was a heated, sweaty cocoon,
He wore three coats, even in June
He didn't go out in winter, not ever
Terrified of snowy weather
His closet was filled with scarves and snow shoes
And coats and gloves in various hues
His parents were worried about his well-being
For the outside world, he was never seeing
But now that winter has finally gone,
Ralph left his house to mow his lawn

Life To Dream
by Yahmin Haj

What is life?
A dream?
So you can feel,
playful like a seal,
to enjoy a meal,
Or to steal?
What is a dream?
Is it a vision?
Or to have enjoyment,
to have unemployment,
To hang out with Mitch,
And feel so rich,
But death will come,
in about some,
days, months, years,
Then approach your fears
But life is a test,
To make your own nest,
You'll be cool in the shade,
For the deeds you made.

What Summer Brings
by Caden Bauer

Summer brings birds and bees
That fly upon the canopies
People going here and there
Breathing in the summer air
With a grizzly bear that wars at night
That brings me the midnight fright

Mondays
by Christian Paramo

The day after Sunday.
It is called a Monday.
It is not a fun-day.
Since it's the start of the weekdays.
It is the cause of much dread.
Since you wish you could stay in bed.
But you have to get up instead.
Which makes you wish you were dead.
You finally get-up.
So you decide to wash-up.
Which helps you wake-up.
Which is the start of your not so fun-day.

The Boy
by Daniel Murray

He walked around the park all day.
He saw the kids laugh and play.
He sat down and started to cry.
A boy sat down and let out a sigh.
The boy said to him, "What is making you sad?"
"I don't know why everyone is so glad."
The boy said, "Why don't you talk to them?"
He walked up to them and said, "Ahem."
The kids turned around and stared.
He was nervous and made a snare.
The kids asked him if he wanted to play.
He had finally made friends and he screamed, "Hooray!"

Dimensions of Me
by George Tjandra

We see a world,
it's like 3 dimensions
from high and below
full of sins and life.
As so long we see this world,
there's even more to see from.
What you say is a way we understand
but some ways we think is peaceful
Each life form has its goal
and that one goal is always you.

Time To Say Goodbye
by Eve Schmidt

You don't see me.
Nobody ever does.
I'm screaming, trying to be heard,
But everyone is deaf to the sound.
Screaming, crying,
Trying to escape.
I'm locked inside a cage
Made of my own feelings.
Somehow, life goes on,
But it's more like just surviving.
I don't want to survive anymore.
It's time to say goodbye.

Wilma Rudolph
by Melina Morrow

Wilma Rudolph, as fast as lightning.
As she runs, she goes so fast.
When she goes by striking,
She knows she won't be last.
As she crosses the finish line,
She feels very divine.
As the crowd cheers on,
She gets her medal at the crack of dawn.
Knowing that she did her best,
She did better than the rest.
Going home with satisfaction,
She gets all of the attraction.

There Is a Meaning To Life
by Cassy Kehs

I don't believe
in the myths people make
and I don't believe
that everything is fake
but I do believe
there's a meaning to life
and that one thing is
Jesus Christ

Lost Creatures
by Dylan Burrows

Dinosaurs, mysteries of the past.
Creatures lost and trapped in time.
There's still a lot to find.
We have bones, teeth, and claws.
As we explore more are discovered.
Some are large and slow,
While others are quick and small.
Dinosaurs varied, no one is better
There are hundreds and hundreds,
Found or waiting to be found.
But the question is,
Will they ever live with us?

The Little Snowflake
by Amy Carvalho

There was a little snowflake sitting in a tree.
The snowflake then decided it wanted to be free.
Once a gust of wind came, the little snowflake fell.
Was it hurt? Was it sad? Nobody could tell.
All the other snowflakes came around to see,
One little snowflake who wanted to be free.
Then a little boy came,
But no one knew his name.
He took all the snowflakes and built them a new house.
They had so much fun, they even rode a mouse.
Then it was time to go back to the tree.
The snowflake then decided it really was free!

No Soccer Practice
by Allison Fu

The rain roars as it plummets down to Earth
Lightning strikes leaving a florescent sky
Thunder blares and the turf jolts beneath me
Now coach declares practice to end tonight.
We all cheer, fists jumping up in the air
Sloppily stuffed bags hang from our shoulders
As we dart down the hill in unison
So jubilant that we don't have practice.
A gush of rain hits me and swarms around,
Donating me a much-needed shower.
I don't care about waiting in the rain,
Because I am fulfilled with gratefulness.
Thanks to Mother Earth, tonight I am free
Of the agonizing soccer practice.

Winter's Last Breath
by Sierra Klug

Winter's last breath
When the air grows warm
Birds start chirping for a late winter's storm
Snow starts falling
When a robin starts calling
The last bit of frost
Then all of winter is lost
Out come the flowers
And all the April showers
Rainbows come out
And the butterflies are about
Hummingbirds and bees
Flowers and green trees
Warm spring days
As we get into the summer phase
Sweet summer fruit
Like coconuts, bananas, and dragon fruit
Winter has melted away
It is time for spring today
Because winter's last breath is done away

Hunting
by Matthew DuBeck

I go in the woods in camo.
I have with me full ammo.
I walk up all the mounds.
Not making a single sound.
I hear a twig snap.
Time to get up from my nap.
I see the buck through the scope.
I am in a stage of hope.
The buck is 40 yards near.
If I miss, I will shed a tear.
I pull the trigger and down he goes.
All night I celebrate with my bros.

Night
by Alex Twery

The whole town is asleep.
even the sheep
go to sleep.
There's not even a peep
or a beep,
nor even a meep
in the town of Kneap.
Not even the birds cheep,
but nearby, frogs leap.
I'd thought they'd be asleep.
They seem to keep
atop a steep
heap.
The tide will sweep.
Stars shine in the deep
purply, grape-colored sky.
Planes fly,
babies cry,
we all wave goodbye.
Wolves howl
and a nearby owl
looks through with a scowl,
and a stench is foul.
It comes from the nearby town, Powwell.
The blue rim of sunrise
Marks the demise
of nighttime.

The Day Under the Willow
by Shripreetika Guruprasad

Prancing under the long branches of the willow tree, no doubt at mind.
The grass tickled, and out came my giggle with a bucket full of joy,
worries that cluttered my head slowly flowed down the river,
into a sea of the forgotten.
The sun smiled through the thin leaves of the willow,
expressing the beauty of spring.
Like butter on toast, a smile spread across my face.
My ears listened to the beautiful tunes of nature,
The birds chirped a cheerful melody, the trees performing a ballet in the wind.
The sky, like a giant canvas was painted a sunset,
The moon spied behind the hill, then rose to confess.
The colorful sky dissolved into a sea of dark blue,
My eyes blinked shut, I floated into a sleep,
After my day under the willow.

Autism, the Unknown
by Kathryn Wright

Most of the time
I think that I know what it feels like
to be looked at like you're crazy
But now, I realize that I don't
and in a million years
I never will
Because when you're no different
from anybody else
You don't notice how hard of a time that they're having
and that their life
was never as easy as our life ever was
So, sometime in your life just notice
that it's a rocky road out there for them
and that you should try and
make it smoother for them
So that our lives
are just the same
–For Autism

Darkest Night
by Donald Smack III

Your body filled with a dreadful chill
Stared at your desk, and the white old quill
Windy night, the quill moved slight
You turned the switch, seeking light.
No light came, the bulb was dead
You thought of going back to bed
Suddenly noticed, the quill moved slight
You approached with all your might
Not the wind, window was closed
Heart raced, a message exposed
You read in horror, ink was red
Not the wind, go back to bed.

The Star of Christmas
by Jhoannie Plegaria

At the darkest time of the night
The star shines its brightest
No matter how thick the clouds are
The presence of a light is guaranteed
This very light is within us all
There is a shine at every open-heart
The warmth of every hug
Will heal every wound of every person
The one who lit this light
Is none other than, you of course
Thank you for your light
Christmas will be colorful once again
We are the light in the dark path
Let us unite even more
Even though we crossed the raging waves
All of us will rise again
Hope will once shine again
Within everyone
Because of you, the one and only son of God
The Star of Christmas

The Swimmer!
by Emily Gudas

You get on the block for your "One Shining Moment."
You dive right in and take one pull.
You kick a few times and there's one almost done.
Then you realize you're not the best one.
You get back in to try again,
You go ahead and repeat the same steps.
Maybe this time you'll actually win,
But instead it is your twin
You try again for the 3rd time.
You have good hopes.
You figure out you're pretty good.
So now that just lightened your mood!

I Am From
by Zahquesz McFadden

When my mom goes out I have to be in the house with my brother and sister.
My mom makes me run to the store
and my mom does not let me play games when I get home.
My mom does not get me what I want
and that is why I do not like going to my mom's house.
When I go to my dad's house he lets me play the game– sometimes.
I like being at my dad's house because I can be on the phone
and I do not have to go to the store,
and I do not have to fight with my brother or sister.
My dad will ask me to come help him do something
and he will let me go to my cousin's house
and I will play the game when I go to his house.
My cousin and I will go outside and play with friends.
My family is a good family to me
but I cannot do a lot because I always have to help somebody in my family.
That's why I like to go to my cousin's house so I can play with my cousin.
His mother does not say a lot to us because we do not do anything bad.
That's why my dad lets me play with him.
He and I do not go to the same school anymore,
but I see him when I go to boxing.
My cousin is funny and that's why I like to go to his house.
My big brother is in jail so he is doing a lot of time.
I miss him, but that does not stop me from going to school.
It's bad because he has kids that are not going to see him for a long time.
My dad is going to help them because they are his son's kids.

The Valiant
by Aaron DiVincezo

The gauntlet has been thrown
as the king laughs on his golden throne.
The valiant breathes deep and draws his sword.
The peoples of the village praise to the almighty lord.
Drops of rain come from the sky.
The kingdom is waiting for a warrior to die.
The heart of the brave one beats even faster.
The loser will be ashamed amidst an uproar of laughter.
The warriors will run towards each other with death in their eyes.
The question is, who will win, who will die?
The crowd goes up, the sword comes down.
The winner is left with the kingdom's crown.

Baseball
by RJ Agriss

I dug my foot into the rubber.
Then, I looked up and remembered
why I love these moments so much.
The yummy smell of the hot dogs,
the look of the green grass.
The smile of the kids' faces,
and the grip of the laces.
So I wound up and pitched
the fastest fastball I could.
Then I looked at the ump,
And what did I see?
I saw his hands go up,
to call strike three.
Our stands went crazy
All our players made a dog pile.
We won the championship!
And we won it in style.

Best Friends
by Jaclyn Jarvis

Friends are forever, they always stick together
Friends are forever, they play and grow together
I'm always on her side, and she is on mine
She's always on my side, even on the fastest ride
We give each other advice, and at mistakes, we pay the price
We don't hold a grudge, and never eat fudge
Friends are forever, we're never in doubt,
You'll see us stick together, without a pout

The Darkness of Ember
by Ella Sharon

It hit me, it hit hard.
The sadness of just finding out.
My heart, it froze and broke into a million pieces.
It was dark, like the black ashes left over from a fire.
My only light was the street lamp.
Flickering, leading me through the darkness of Ember.
I felt evil swarming me.
Taking every single, bad thing,
making me feel guilty.
Walking through the cold.
Lightning struck, and thunder stormed.
I kept my eyes closed.
Thinking if it was my fault.
I listened to the rain,
plink! plink!
Tears rolling down my cheeks.
Catching the rhythm of the rain.
I kept my head down.
Letting my hair soak up my tears.
I finally looked up.
I followed the alleyway and found a peek of light,
at the end of the tunnel.

Colors
by Livi Hadzick

Red is like a big red rose
Orange is like the refreshing taste of orange Sunkist soda
Yellow is like the daffodils in my front yard
Green is like the green waving grass in the summer breeze
Blue is like the big blue summer sky
Purple is like the soothing smell of lavender
Pink is like the juicy taste of bubblegum
White is like the slippery white ice in the winter time
Black is like the black midnight sky

Narnia, My Home
by Jonathon Bernet-Aponte

Once I read *The Chronicles of Narnia* series
And when I finished the series I had many dearies
For the series ended
And my friends stayed, the friends I have friended
And the adventures we had, we were really glad
And some of the adventures were sad
In *The Magician's Nephew* we saw Narnia when it began
I meet Digory, Polly, the Pegasus, Jadis the witch, Andrew Ketterley, and Aslan
Then in *The Lion, The Witch, and The Wardrobe* we defeated the witch
Lucy, Edmund, Peter, Susan, Mr. Tumnus, Mr. and Mrs. Beaver, and also the witch
In the book *The Horse and His Boy* we saw the four runaways go to Narnia
There was Aslan, Bree and Hwin the horses, the Pevensies,
Rabadash, and also Shasta
And in the next book *Prince Caspian*, we helped Caspian become the king
Prince Caspian, Reepicheep the mouse, Trumpkin the Badger,
the Pevensies, Miraz the king.
In *The Voyage of the Dawn Treader* we sailed to the utter East and the country
of Aslan. Caspian, Edmund, Lucy, Eustace, Reepicheep, Ramandu the wizard,
the seven Lords, and Aslan
In *The Silver Chair* we saved Prince Rilian in the Underworld
Prince Caspian, Eustace, Jill Pole, Puddleglum, Aslan,
and the Lady of the Green Kirtle
Then the last book of all, *The Last Battle*,
where we saw Narnia come to its final end.
Aslan, Peter, Lucy, Edmund, Digory, Eustace, Jill, Caspian,
Shasta, Tirian, and animal friends.

Summertime
by Samantha Maar

Super
Unforgettable
Magic
Memory
Everlasting
Realistic
Timeless
Incredible
Magnificent
Everlasting

A Survivor
by Emma Thiel

Started teaching dance at a young age.
Unbelievable courage while fighting cancer.
Resilient about getting back to where she was.
Vibrant; always teaching with a hop in her step and a smile on her face.
Inspiration to others; showing how to be strong and always think positive.
Very positive, giving us praise and pushing us forward.
Offers time, talent, and advice to others.
Runner– cancer can't stop her!

Gray Whale
by Megan Brady

Ginormous fins
Rhythmic, moving swiftly with the currents
Adventurous creatures
Yapping excitedly to one another

Wandering into the outstretched arms of awaiting waters
Hunting heartily, hushed until just the right moment comes along
Acrobatic animals
Luxuriously leaping, breaching, flying out of the water
Excitedly breaking the ocean's salty surface,
            and plunging back into its mysterious depths

In the Moment
by Daniel Kaplan

Cherish today, tomorrow might not be
Spend time with those who you truly hold dearly
It could all be different when you wake up
You could be needed to be a grown up
Live every day as though it is your last
Live for today, but remember the past.
Accomplish all your deepest desires
Even if you couldn't achieve them prior
Don't dwell on what you've previously done
Live with no regrets and have tons of fun
If there's something that you ever missed out on
You make the most of it before it's gone
Because you never know when time is over
Take risks and don't wait for a four-leaf clover

Warmth
by Isaac John

The warmth I feel is the warmth I steal,
not like a thief, but like a child,
who steals the hearts of others,
the child who steals the hearts of mothers.

You Are My Weakness
by Leslie Ventura-Soto

My love for him is inevitable.
Started like a fire and now cannot be stopped.
How did this start? Such feelings I have for him
and he doesn't even know who I am.
Love can cross borders but sometimes cannot reach its destination.
He is like the heavens,so angelic, but I cannot touch him.
I am desperate now but nobody notices.
He is looking at her, but not me. How can that be?
How can I live without his love?
I cannot leave this love behind because I know that someday he is going to realize
I was there the whole time but he was too foolish to notice.
My love for him will never die because my love for him is so wild and yet so tinid
but it cannot be stopped.
I will wait a hundred years for him.
Just please remember me.

Midnight Fireflies
by Justen Frisch

every night I lay awake
and every now and then I see a firefly full of wonder, just like me
how can you not see the possibilities
every night when I go to sleep, the fireflies go to eat
every morning when I wake, the fireflies go away

Bob's Cockatiel Birds
by Sage Smith

Buddy and Petty are two Cockatiel birds
Who really like to talk
And are always walking up
And down their long flight of stairs.
They are grey and white, with spiky hair and
Cheeks that look like blush,
They always fight with each other
But they are never alone and always tough.
When Buddy and Petty were eating
A strange thing happened to them
A crow came down to eat them
But he ran into a window.

Fantastical Addiction
by Adessa McDougall

Part of me is bewildered teal.
Insecure and Ignored.
Impatient and Vengeful.
Stewing without retaliation,
Brewing the sadness inside.
But deep inside there is another part,
Rich lime, like a Leprechaun gone wrong.
Competent and wild.
Nerdy and nutty.
A giddy fangirl nursing the high of a mind-blowing epiphany.
Both of these sides of me are very real,
Each yearning for a quirkier reality

Gillian Perrotta

Falling Into Life
by Gillian Perrotta

The leaf slowly drifts down from the brightly lit tree,
Its colors a deep red, and fiery orange.
I imagine that I am that leaf,
So beautiful, so graceful.
Like a ballerina, twirling and leaping,
I dance my way through the air.
Each gust of wind, each new path I take,
A new experience, I gain knowledge.
By the end of my breathtaking ride,
I am like a wise old soul.
While I am turning brown, and wrinkling on the outside,
I am full of wisdom, and bold colors, and joy.
At the end of my journey,
I am old, but I am new.
I'm not just another green leaf on the tree,
Or another brown haired, green eyed girl in the world.
I am unique, just like the blazing leaf I catch in my palm.
Its life is almost over,
and a promising green bud will soon take its place on the tree.
I stuff the leaf in my pocket, and continue walking down the forest path.
While its journey has ended, mine has just begun.

Elaine Yang

Ambush
by Elaine Yang

Our secret battlefield was in my brother's room, no adults allowed.
The door was closed, the blinds shut tight, all the lights were off.
We huffed and we puffed
as we pushed the beds into the farthest corners of the room.
Big, heavy comforters hid the beds from sight,
Propped up by pillows and cold bed frames standing guard.
Pillows were stepping stones carving paths around booby traps,
Stuffed animals were hostages shivering beneath the covers.
Huddled under a big green blanket,
we would formulate a plan of attack together.
We would peek out at the enemy base to find the chinks in their armor.
As we wrapped our invisibility cloaks around ourselves
and wished each other luck,
We would hear the enemy's thunderous cry, "To victory!"
All of a sudden,
The enemy was upon us, furiously tickling us,
and whipping away the blankets.
We would glare fiercely at your brother
marching, across the trampled path of pillows,
Carrying the freed hostages above his head like trophies.
My brother would lift the edge of their blue blanket,
allowing him to enter their camp.
Your brother would sweep inside, blue cape trailing behind.
You and I would lie limply on the bed, silently watching the ceremony,
Defeated for the moment, but craving revenge.

1st Place

Fisher Boyd

This 6th grader's poem is one of our favorites,
and while we don't know what or who is the inspiration,
we are fairly certain that like its hero,
its author must be eccentric and smart
with a great sense of humor.
Well done!

Nerd
by Fisher Boyd

Maybe I do stay up late till my eyes shut on their own,
Reading, sometimes a book for the eighteenth time.
So what if I care about my grades
And they're above average
I'm proud of it
So, go ahead and shout, "Nerd!"
Across the hallway at me
I'll wear it as a title
And I'll be proud of it!
Wow, you stumped me
I still can't figure out
Why you would think that a word that I find complimenting
Would be used
As ammunition,
As an insult
Why would you think of it as a degrading put-down
For I find it as an honor
To carry around a badge that tells people that I am eccentric and smart.
But honestly,
I prefer, "Geek"

Division III

Grades 8~9

The Dude Named Jude
by Parker Simmons

There once was a dude named Jude
Who was really quite very rude
One day while he raked
He was put in an oven and baked
Well after that he was no longer rude

Best Friend
by Ashley Beasley

Best friend ...
The one who is always there to encourage
Best friend ...
The one who is always there to pick up
Best friend ...
The one who is always there to share a smile
Share a laugh, share a talk
Best friend ...
For you I can depend and when I am around you I do not have to pretend
You know my flaws and all of my weaknesses
You know my story and even my past
Best friend ...
You are my first good morning and my last goodnight
We always stick together even in our fights
You are my first hello and my last goodbye
Without you I cannot discover which days will shine
Best friend ...
We are so much more ...
We know we have each other's back and that is for sure
Side by side and back to back
We face our fears together and we get back on track
You correct my wrong and I correct yours
We have a way of doing it without causing a war
Best friend ...
You are special to me and I am special to you
That makes us the perfect fit in life
and one big Dream Come True!!

Let Happiness Grow
by Daysia Harris

Along the beaten paved road is where my past lay
the days of sorrow and the days of pain
Where nighttime sadness followed to the day
Where my world was always surrounded in rain
But these days were soon over when I would sit in grief
I could not do it anymore
I had to let go of all disbelief
I had to take a risk and face my chances
So I faced the fears and left sadness' trances
Opportunities await for brighter tomorrow
No more days of pain and sorrow
No more rain and storm clouds, only the sun's ray
Oh how thankful I am for that one life-changing day
The day I decided to let it all go
The day I decided to let happiness grow.

Coffee
by Leah Roy

Again that cup sitting on the table,
filled with good, pleasurable coffee for me.
Although it tastes good it is unable
to keep my teeth clean or let it be free.
Coffee is not better than nice smiles,
for nice smiles represent a person.
A smile can have different styles.
This should always teach someone a lesson.
Smiles can't satisfy a stomach though.
For only coffee can do that simply.
Coffee will not let your body go low.
Just the essence will wake you up quickly.
There is no other thing better than this.
For coffee is just goodness and pure bliss.

Almost Finished
by Anthony Hands

Nine months passed and it's time to go,
All the time we've had to learn more and grow
No more turtlenecks, golf shirts and sweaters,
It's just how I imagined it, maybe even better
All the friendships made, times good and bad,
Even the fights that we seldom had
But now that's history, it's come to an end,
Now the real fun is about to begin
Time to go to high school and make some new friends,
Start a new journey that in four years will end
I loved the time I spent at Lab, don't get be wrong,
But things come and go, all you have to do is move along
I will never forget this school, I've had so much fun,
But playtime is over and the jokes are done
It's all over now, more room for learning,
Hope we all succeed as we embark on a brand new journey

Lost In the Book
by Trinity Anglesey

I'm not spellbound
Just nowhere to be found
Mentally I'm here
But physically I'm there
I'm lost in my fairy tale
Spinning in details
I feel their feelings
Even if they're revealing
This book I hold
Its story is mold
My mind ventures far
About everything and all
The stories are on my mind
Like we are bound with time
I get deeper and deeper
Steeper and steeper
I thought I wasn't lost
But didn't know the cost
Unaware that I was lost in this book

If We Could Hear Them
by Kristin Kelley

If we could hear the whispers of the trees,
Would we listen?
If animals could tell how much they were hurting,
Would we try harder to help?
If the wind was able to tell its purpose,
Would we care?
Why the pesky weeds just never give way,
Why all the leaves just blow away,
Would we stop cutting trees?
Would all the animals be loved and helped,
And wind, weeds, and leaves not complained about?
Would we listen to what they had to say?
Maybe not, because people speak too.

Gone
by Keiana Palmer

Week before, so I was with you
We were outside and the flowers were new
Your pure heart beating so loud
I hugged you and I heard it pound
You were always there for me
You saw things no one else could see
Always noticing my ambition
I'd come to you and you'd listen
You are my hero, a diamond in the rough
I knew being without you would be tough
One Four Three is 8. meaning infinity
I'd wish you stayed so you could see what I'd be
It was the last time I heard your heart
You said you loved me and the tears would start
I always knew it, never had to guess
That the person who stood before me was the best
The next week I've heard the news
I was terribly sad and terribly blue
You'd left me and it felt so wrong
Because the greatest cousin I knew was now GONE!
– Dedicated to Devon Johnson

Moments of Life
by Tia Hammond

Have you ever had that moment,
Where time has ever stopped?
Where everyone was looking at you,
Like you were the crazy one?
Faces are dark,
They are all around you
But all you see are the whites of their teeth.
Spreading rumors is their specialty.
Being fake is their life.
Being nice is a disease.
Living my life is a pain
In a world of black and white
My world doesn't spin
My body is empty shell
No emotions are evident
No smile lights up my face.
Just an empty life,
Waiting to end.

Two Parts of Me
by Lilly Nuxoll

There two parts of me
You rarely get to see.
Here I will explain but you must read carefully.
Part of me is very light green,
Soft and sweet,
But hidden in fear of
Being different from the rest.
But looking farther there's another part.
It's deep red and full of heart,
Bravery, strength, and smarts,
Compassion and courage
All belong to this part to make it whole.
You barely see this side of me,
Like a river black sky,
With a moon darker than dragon's blood,
And its luminating light could make rain look
Like droplets of falling blood.

The Punishment
by Mekenzie Hill

I never knew the punishment.
pain, sorrow, rage.
you carry the anger of an army,
the fear of a raging fire,
and the haunting wails of the wind.
you're an outcast, like the shadows of the forest.
but worst of all; is the hatred.
the foul feeling that grows without you every day.
consuming the joy, love, and life you once possessed.
gone.
now ... you're all alone.
The kind of courage you have to forge to be alone.
in these dark woods ... is a painful task.
but the punishment has been given.
no turning back.
no running away.
no way to escape it.
you have forever become ...
a werewolf.

The Most Peaceful Place On Earth
by Darian Clark

The oak fresh smell fills your nostrils when you enter a trail,
A slow moving stream, next to you, has a deer drinking calmly at,
The soft dirt under your feet squishes after each step,
The tall, green oak trees sway in the wind giving you a breeze,
A small crack of a nut, to make you look up,
To see a squirrel enjoying a meal,
As the train bends corners, a cliff is now beside you,
A breath of the fresh open air fills you with relaxation,
When a bald eagle soars over your head to catch prey,
The fog just lifting off the mountain gives you a clear view,
Of a creek flowing at the bottom of the cliff,
The silver and gold fish swimming upstream,
Gives you the sign of peace, calm, and unwinding feeling,
Just when you think to turn and continue on the trail,
You get a hungry feeling, so you stop to eat,
A crunchy granola bar to give you energy and zest,
Until a loud snap of a tree branch makes you turn right,
To see a large, brown elk staring into your eyes,
Slowly, not to disturb the peaceful animal, you keep walking down the trail,
Until you realize, you're at the end of the most peaceful place on Earth.

Rain
by Dylan Wilkins

Rain falls upon my face
Wet against my skin
The storm rages on the outside
But also from within.
My tears won't stop flowing
The pain I can no longer hide
I'll have to fight this battle–
Without you by my side.

Her Emotions
by Gabby Massaro

Every single night,
she lays in her bed,
wondering about the things
going on in her head.
Sometimes she was happy,
sometimes she was sad
even though people said
her life wasn't that bad.
When she was happy,
her smile was as bright as the sun,
and all she wanted to do
was have fun.
When she was sad,
some compared her to the rain,
dark, cold, grey,
but she was filled with pain.
Her emotions could be compared
to the currents out at sea,
but that was who
she eventually came to be.
So even though sometimes,
her emotions gained power,
she was still as beautiful
as a field of flowers.

The Pulchritudinous Things
by Isabella Galante

A heart is punctured with small gashes from these thorns
thousands of petals cascade down your cheek
Being gradually aggrieved
inconsiderable fragments of you go astray
which are kept
which are disposed of.
How am I picked, adored, thrown away.
Take all of my petals, go on ahead
just make sure you take the rest of me.
No one acquires the petals without the thorns
If you are pricked, don't change your mind.
I am now so distant from my garden.
Water me and whisper words to help me respire.
Without you I'll wilt, be my new garden.

The Lonely Girl
by Hannah Nolt

The little girl sits there in the night,
Without a family or friend in sight.
She holds a candle in her hand;
With a little flicker of the light.
No one seems to care,
That she is lying there cold and bare.
But she is not alone;
Jesus is there.
She felt so betrayed,
And that made her afraid.
But she prayed to Jesus,
For He says He will never leave us.
She remembers her prayer,
And says to herself,
This is a prayer to keep;
And then falls asleep.
She dreams of a day,
When she can share her prayer.
And can be His servant;
To the lost and hurting souls everywhere.

Earth's Tumor
by Normen Yu

One mutation:
That is how we get cancer
One mutation:
That is what created human
Wouldn't you think
Earth and us are just so alike?
How do you think
The Earth is likely going to end?
Shouldn't we think
That we could find a compromise?
A compromise
That we should all contribute to?

Silence
by Jamal Hughes, Jr.

I am silenced like all the black boys and girls, so I'm not alone.
Black men should be on a throne, but we're nowhere near the castle.
We stay silent.
I can't speak unless it's through my cheek.
My mom asked why.
I reply I don't want to become another statistic of these animalistic murders.
Why are we fighting?
Why does the neighborhood park have to be a warzone?
Why can't we call this city our own?
We are silent because something our ancestors had beaten into their
subconscious, don't speak unless spoken to.
Don't speak unless it's something they want to hear.
Why are we so afraid of the people who are supposed to protect and serve?
How were we ever supposed to believe a system set against us would ever
protect and serve?
Liberty and justice for who?
Because it can't be us, they left us in the dust
This world taught me never to trust.
We stay silent because silence is our defense mechanism against this system
full of errors.
There is no hope for peace, no hope for us being able to walk
without looking behind and that's why we can't move forward.
They want us to be silent but I can't, I won't
My voice has been caged for too long
It's about time for it to be free.

Imagine
by Kendra Thatcher

A cloud floats beside me,
I jump into its mysterious shape,
Thoughts begin to rush through me,
My imaginary friends of old appear,
Games of long ago come to life,
I slowly drift into an insane dream,
Animals begin to talk to me,
Rain begins to sing to me,
Snow begins to dance with me,
I begin to float towards the sky,
I fly with birds and slowly hit the ground again,
Suddenly I wake up finding myself in my old clubhouse,
Looking around me I see all the toys I used to play with,
I carefully pick up an old friend,
Timmy the teddy bear,
My imagination has finally found me again

Part of the Team
by Ryan Burns

Being part of a team is more than the outside shows.
It is more than just showing up to practice.
It is more than just putting on a jersey and playing a sport.
It is about dedicating yourself to your team.
And about putting effort into every move that you make.
It is about owning up to your mistakes.
And supporting your teammates in every way possible.
It is about keeping a positive attitude throughout all situations.
And trying your hardest through easy and tough times.
It is about maintaining good sportsmanship.
No matter if you win or lose.
No matter what the case may be.
Every time you put on your jersey.
You are representing your team.
If you wear your jersey with pride.
And give 110% effort.
You just may have what it takes, to be a part of the team.

Life Is Good and Life Is Bad
by Andrew Iannacone

Life isn't always as you will want it to be,
there are twists and turns,
ups and downs,
and dead ends.
Sometimes life is bright,
and sometimes life is dark,
but whichever one you're in,
you should always be happy.
You can choose what to do with your life,
because you are free,
and you, no one can tell you what to do,
because you are free.

Peace, God, and the Human Bane
by Izzy Newnam

I save children, see:
I take away the bruises and thirst and raw need
the paranoia, anxiety, and coveted greed
the black expression all in their head
the incessant buss of voices long since dead
I don't believe in him:
he is a figure to blame
a deity, interposed between his shades of fame
but yet he knows it, knows what I've done
if he catches me, his war is won
he most think me cruel:
some girl too young
shoes too big, disposition too snug
he thinks I sit complacently on my throne
like the devil herself, has finally come home
and yet he is not wrong
because
the children that I had once saved
were put to rest in shallow graves
by the same hands who brought release,
me, and my cold, deep, empty peace.

On Turning
by Ben Helzner

They may say it's not too bad,
but right now I'm feeling worse
than any cut could hurt,
worse than any fire burns.
It's a stabbing of the conscience,
a tearing of the soul.
They may say it's not too bad,
what I've done is excusable.
But when I think upon it,
There's a sadness much too deep,
To ever heal completely.
They may say it's not too bad,
but I ask, do they remember
the first time they hurt someone?
Truly hurt them,
so much so they remember
more than blowing out their birthday candles,
more than turning ten?

He Picked Me
by Kassidy Moore

At the thought of you
I smile
At the sight of you
I cringe
And yet I want to meet you
No matter what
You are my idol
The one and only
The one that knows everything that there is to know
The one and only
That I'd love to impress
Because you impress me each and every day
When you judge me
My heart is in the sky
So high it can't be drug down
When you pick me
It soars even higher
When night comes I can't sleep
Because my cheeks hurt from smiling
He picked ME

Volleyball
by Paige Gunter

Volleyball is a game where you can get your anger out.
Volleyball is a game where you can hit someone and not get in trouble for it.
Volleyball is a game where you can call something and everyone backs off.
Volleyball is a game when the ball comes over the net and everyone is saying mine
and you sound like the fish on Finding Nemo.
But most of all volleyball is a game where you can have fun.

Eric Thomas, Yesterday, Today, Tomorrow
by Brenner Adams

Lived on the cold streets,
From the time he was born,
But he never quit.
Hasn't given up,
Opens his steel umbrella,
When the rain falls hard.
He'll be at the top,
Until the day that he dies,
It's Eric Thomas.

A Rose
by Emily O'Malley

A rose is a way to express yourself.
When you give a flower to a person you care about,
Think of its meaning.
Red means love, courage, and passion.
White means respect and heavenly.
Pink means thank you and graceful.
Yellow means joy and delight.
Orange means friendship.
Peach means appreciation.
And lavender means happiness.
The meaning is worth more than the flower itself.

The Better Hero
by Jeremy Capella

Spiderman
Cool, popular
Web slinging, wall climbing, death defying
Avengers, Justice League
Justice bringing, Gotham protecting, cape wearing
Dark, ninja
Batman

I Will Smile Again
by Felecia Richey

I will smile again
Though tears flow from these eyes.
I will smile again
And trust that tomorrow the sun shall rise!
Though darkness may enfold me
Though heavy rain can't help but pour
Though shattered, lost and broke
I will smile again!
Though my heart could hardly bear it all
Though tired, weary and confused
Though badly hurt and bruised
I know that I will smile again
And I will smile again!

The Desert of Life
by Angelina Toole

A lonely hyena bellows atop a hill, as the sun rises behind him.
Rays of the sun radiate onto the sandy landscape before him.
Tall emus stand proudly, gradually lowering themselves to the dry earth.
Pecking impatiently at the lifeless ground, searching for beetles and water.
Snakes and lizards hiss at the noise of approaching prey.
A land untouched conceals its inhabitants from the world.
The sandy dunes unseen by man are shrouding the exotic creatures.
Cactus flowers bloom in the scorching heat.
Animals manage to carry on their lives,
without knowing man's plans to corrupt its beauty.

The Transition From Autumn To Spring
by Amanda Lanzillo

Autumn
Breeze, foggy
Hibernating, harvesting, rustling
Raking leaves, smelling flowers
Blossoming, awakening, chirping
Colorful, rainy
Spring

Books and Movies
by Austin Orbin

Books
Pages, writing
Reading, imagining, picturing
Flipping pages, pausing scenes
Watching, directing, acting
Suspenseful, big-budget
Movies

Slenderman
by Natasha Guevara

Frowned upon was he,
Man with glistening skin.
At night he came,
And turned away,
For fear he might be caught.
Encased in his arms,
Will cause quite a fright.
You kick and you scream,
And fight for your life.
You searched for the map,
That would lead you home,
But instead you were captured,
Within his Slender-Dome.

Light and Darkness
by Richie Pospiech

Light
Bright, luminous
Sunshine, starlight, bulb
Day transitions into night
Shadows, twilight, murky
Black, gloom
Darkness

Silence
by Oliver H. Hunter V

The silence of the outside world,
Shattered by the simplicity of sound,
Silence is never achieved,
Unless isolated from the rest of the world,
Lost in a deep slumber,
Separated from all that happens.

She Who Is Also Me
by Sierra Silvestro

Who is this person?
With eyes so large.
With hands so small.
With a halo hanging upon her crown?
Who is this person?
With a pristine glow, a gaping mouth, and a creased brow.
Who studies her other half with the focus of a searchlight
locating a troubled criminal
and the intensity of the sun beating upon the Earth in early July.
Who is this person so close, yet so far?
Why does she share the same ranging brown focus, freckled arms,
and tiny figure with another?
As a small mind questions, so does that of the reflection in the mirror.

Rainbows
by Giana Melfe

An organized array, the light of day,
With tears of clouds glitters the tranquil sky
It paints the heavens, divine songs display
The colors stretch around the world, a dye.
How lovely now here stands the arch of life
The sign of promise, God to all He gave
A manifestation from man, housewife
To creatures God from massive floods He'll save
But some believe in pots of lucent gold
A superstition, day and night a light
Must race their way to treasure they've been told
Contains transcendence, comes with power, fight!
Don't run with them for you will find the seed
That grows in hearts; the seed soon turns to greed.

A Broken Band
by Jacob DeTreux

When the lights were on and shining
We were met by greeting hands
Having a good time rocking out
Back when we were in a band
Blasting guitars and banging drums
Making songs was our life's plan
But now we are nobodies since
Back when we were in a band
The stadiums are now ghost towns
The signs filled with our old brands
But the memories remind us
Back when we were in a band
Speakers turned as loud as lions
With songs as sweet as candy
Making songs was our life's plan
Back when we were in a band
The tour bus was old and smelly
The seats like sitting on sand
But it got us from place to place
Back when we were in a band
Then one day the bad news came
Next thing I knew I was canned
The band said that I was like a jerk
Back when we were in a band

Wiping Tears
by Baylee Hess

What are you waiting for? Jump up off that floor.
Wipe those tears away then we can be on our way.
What, you're not going? Those tears just keep a showing.
Fine, I'll stay here with you, there is no need to argue.
The time will fly right by. And I? I will be your only ally. No goodbyes.
So have you changed your mind since I've been so kind.
What are you waiting for? Let's open that door.
Those tears are gone anyway. That smile is making its way.
I guess we're going. That smile is just a glowing.
You don't need to be blue. All you need is to be you!

The Ultimate Sacrifice
by Zachary Schrag

In Darkness,
I came to be.
Born here, to live happy and free.
I met my sibling in my new home
And I soon had more brothers to call my own.
I went to school and made some friends,
My mother said she was not sad, but it was just pretend.
I soon grew up and came to be,
The man my father was proud to see.
I left the house and like a worker bee, I found a hive to work in glee.
Then The War came from afar,
And we all were drafted, soon to know,
The blood and horror that war will show.
And into battle we were thrown
To shoot and kill, though we didn't know
Who we killed or why we did.
But they did the same, and eventually it came.
The gun had rendered me heartless,
And then, right there
Behind the lines, full of despair, I suddenly was
In Darkness.

Spy?
by Seth Cram

Are you just a spy
When you ask but not give aid
Looking into my eyes
But then will I have it made?
When you find what's really inside
Or will you lead me to my grave

A Shakespearian Tragedy
by Emma Rose Berrier

At the end of my life,
The credits read tragedy.
In the last blink of my eye,
Your face crosses my mind,
I go back to that day,
When I was happy,
Because I had you,
The two of us,
But it was never me and you,
It was just me,
Left alone in a Shakespearian Tragedy

Judgment Day
by Andy Nguyen

The smell of burning flesh
Screams of fear all and around
Tears of salvation
The light by which people are taken straight
Towards Heaven
Running like there are no means of tomorrow
Prayers towards God
To grant them a passage to Heaven
Everybody as they say goodbye
While enjoying their lives as they can.
Devastation of dead bodies
Thieves, as they take as much as they can before it all ends
As if you didn't know
But this is Judgment Day
Where the end appears near.

Wind
by Amanda Hansell

It blew softly,
It blew fast,
It sounded sharp,
When it passed.
Oh, wonderful wind,
The things it can do,
It blows away trees,
Or houses, or shoes.
It feels good on the skin,
It blows through your hair.
Wind is amazing,
Yet is only air.
The sounds, the feelings
Of wind everywhere,
Are so fascinating,
I declare.

Separation: a Holocaust Remembrance Poem
by Daja Hosendorf

The distance is undesirable
It's like someone pulling a rubber band at each end
Then cutting it in the middle
We are separated by force
Not by choice
As we drift away from each other,
It's hard to be away from one another
I'm not sure if there is a way to bring us back together
They tell us ...
"Women to the right, men to the left"
Will I ever see my mother again?
Shivers
They run up and down and through my body
It's like the first time stepping in an ice-cold bath
These chills I feel
Are from the loneliness instilled
I'm told to stand tall and be a man
But I want to be a boy
Still in my mother's hands

Holocaust
by Yaamir Dillard

Taken away!
Shattered!
All hope and faith slowly fade away.
Dreams of freedom begin to fade, like a shadow in the shade.
Families were ripped apart and never seen again, like a leaf drifting in the wind.
Fear, takes over the mind and soul,
It leaves people all alone.
Glorious days were on the way, American forces came to save the day.
People, so overjoyed by the sound of freedom,
didn't know whether or not to believe them.
Restored!
Returned, the faith and hope of all the people!
The Holocaust was finally over, and the Jews could all rejoice.

For Her
by Gabrielle Bioteau

I'm not walking
To clear my head or to lose some weight
I'm not just walking
I'm saving lives and I'm raising awareness
I'm doing this for her
Her smile flashes before my eyes
Her voice rings in my ears
Her touch spreads across my skin
I'm doing this for her
I wear a pink shirt and a pink tutu and a pink wristband that says hope
Hope was all she had
Hope was all she could have
Hope didn't save her
But I have her spirit and I have her hope
I'll save her fighting spirit
In all the others like her; in all the other fighters
So I'm not just walking
To clear my head or to lose some weight
I'm doing this
For her

Rain
by Karly Smith

She lies in bed
listening to the water
Fall from the sky
it makes her strangely
happy inside
the lightning struck
and the thunder roared
she stared out the window
as the rain pours
The thunder roared so loudly
it shook the house
frightening even the little mouse
The lightning strikes oh so bright
leaving the beautiful sky with lights

Ode To Teachers
by Darlina Chavez

Since I was little
You were always there
To teach me everything, even riddles.
Without you I'd be dumb
The thoughts are so scary
I can't imagine writing
Without you helping
You're always there
When I need you
I'll just raise my hand
And I'll see you
You're sweeter than my taffy
You always make me happy
You come to school
Your hair is not nappy
Teachers full of joy
Everything you do shows you care
You look happy teaching girls and boys
I can see it in your stare

Ode To Reading
by Siera Hicks

I'm bored and decide to relax
Reading is something that should keep me on track
As I'm reading all I can see and feel are words
They are dancing to the silent chirps of birds
The mood of the story makes me shiver
The shiver runs down my spine like a stream and a river
I'm finished reading the book and choose to stare
To stare about the adventures that took place in there
I love to read because it takes me to a place I can't go
It expresses the feelings I can't show
I'm bored again and decide to relax
Reading is something that will keep me on track

Turning Tides
by Annamay Hartbauer

At this thing called life we try to get to the crown
but it will wind up leaving you with a really big frown
'Cause tides turn and waves crash
Fire burns and turns to ash
We may not see the road ahead
Still don't look back or you will dread
Never stray from your path of gold
or you will pay a hefty toll
Mischievous things lie beyond
struggles, hardships, all for a cause
But things get better, yes indeed
you may even try to leave
Just don't stop, believe
Just open your heart and open your mind
to receive the encouragement of others you left behind
Things will get hard and very brutal
Just know the world is still beautiful.

Summertime
by Caroline Zieba

Summertime is on its way.
Summer is the time to play.
but, for now I'm still in school,
only dreaming of the pool.
The days go by so slowly now,
I have a frown upon my brow.
If only break would come much sooner
I'd ditch the books and the tutor.
All day long I'd play outside.
In this state I would preside,
eating foods like watermelon
and feeling like the great Magellan.
My days would be so homework free
and my life would fill with glee.
Summer is the time for fun
and lying in the nice warm sun.
When the summertime has ended,
by then my spirits will be mended,
and back to school then I will go
to learn what I do not yet know.

The Day I Started Football
by Cole Kramer

The hot gridiron rose up to meet our cleats
its turf and grass an afterthought across which we ran,
working in an intense summer heat where no other life existed
beyond the sideline of the field.
Shaking off the sweat from our heads,
we lifted dummies and tackling bags along the track around the field.
Hungry and tired, we ate and slept until practice again that night,
lifted weights to the beat of "Turn Down for What".
Popcorn, ham sandwiches, Landhope Lemonade,
we walked to the field where gnats followed around our heads and in our eyes.
We gulped gallons of water that was as cold as ice,
sitting under trees in the shade. Maple, oak, yellow birch.
We spread our helmets on the field, pressed ice packs to our heads,
Mouthing the pain from bruises, then loosened bulky football pads
and pressed cold wet towels across burning necks,
tossing a glance to the parking lot at a world filled with homework that night.
– Inspired by "The Summer I Turned Sixteen" by Geraldine Connolly

School ... Drool
by Kayla D'Agostino

I have clothes to match;
A bus to catch.
People to see,
Places to be,
Then food to eat;
A bell to beat.
I got classes to attend;
Information to comprehend.
Soft and gentle wind,
Blow me away like a delicate leaf;
Lay me down in a bed of grass.
Bright and luminous sun,
Shine your rays on me;
Light up the sky
Clear drops of rain,
Fall on my hot skin;
Cool me down

Pretty White Horses Prancing
by Brooke Chase

Her mind was crazy as ever
Peering at clouds shaped like feathers
Dreaming of unicorns dancing
And pretty white horses prancing
Not knowing anything was wrong
Life continued on just as strong
Dreaming of fairies enchanting
and pretty white horses prancing
But then many needles stuck her
and Sam wasn't any better
Her little curls kept bouncing
She dreamt of white horses prancing
Chemo had her in a lil' funk
But St. Jude doctors kept her spunk
Luckily she kept advancing
And dreamed of white horses prancing.

Sleep
by Edgar Gaspar

Sleep is essential
Even if we don't need it all of the time
we still find time
is great time passer
Having happy dream
Having a nightmare
Having nothing
Whatever it is you forget in an instant
in the night is just right
in the morning great
in the afternoon sure
Then do it all over again

Blue Morning Light
by Calissa Jacobson

I wake to pale blue morning light slipping through my bedroom window,
and the breeze rustling through the trees.
I slip out of bed, pitter-patter down the hall, and open the front door.
I immediately feel the cool, pure breeze.
The morning light is beginning to be whisked away through the air.
I look towards the almost sunrise.
The chill of morning blows through my hair.
I am speechless.
The sun has not even begun to rise, but I feel whole inside.
The blue grass of my backyard shimmers with dew.
The pale blue sky looks so open and wide.
I step onto the damp ground. My bare toes tingle in the wet, cool grass.
I take a deep breath, taking in the light of early morning,
the fresh cool air, the quiet birds, and the silky breeze.
Then ... I run.
Between the trees, over the chilling grass, by the old tractor.
I glance at the dandelions as I pass.
Suddenly, I stand completely still.
Sun rays burst over the horizon.
When dawn comes, it all starts again, only in different light and life.

Looks Real, But Look Closer
by Alondra Camacho

Looks real
a new trend of
photorealistic painting
shocking lucidity
but look closer
— Inspired by "Looks Real But Look Closer" from New York Times

Lost Home
by Sophia Ruggio

One lost home.
Left it for better.
Years go on.
Never thinking of it.
Till one day,
That house goes away.
Burnt to the ground.
The thought of the house,
Realizing all of those memories
Are left behind.
My one lost home.

Earth
by Cristian Flores

Earth is where we live,
Where we laugh and have fun
Where we get sad.
Earth is our home.
A blue and green sphere that spins around the bright hot sun,
Earth is warm, cold, sandy, or grassy green.
Earth can be anything,
It may seem small
But it is quite big.
It is home to billions of lives.
For billions of years we had the honor to call Earth our home.
We may destroy it, but some of us try to save it.
We may succeed or fail trying.
But Earth will always be our home.

His Universe
by Emma Kail

Normal rules don't apply
Most popular cosmologist of the past century
Severe case of
Lou Gehrig's disease
Rare scientific luminary
"A Brief History of Time"
His Oxford student days
Illness was diagnosed
First marriage
His science
No shy and retiring genius
Stephen Hawking
– Inspired by "The Brilliance of His Universe" from New York Times.

Life
by Zachary Eich Woodward

Life is what we have
Life is what the plants have
Life is when you have to wake up early in the morning
Life is the air you breathe
Life is when you dance to your favorite song
Life is when you go to church
Life is how long it takes until church ends
Life is when we play sports
Life is the way our bodies work
Life is when we eat, sleep and drink
Life is the time you spend with your family
Life is your job
Life is our country
Life is the way we live
The way we live is life

Ode To Family
by Sydney Shumaker

My family is huge.
It includes,
2 grandparents, 5 aunts, 4 uncles,
17 cousins, 12 second cousins,
1 third cousin, 5 cousins-in-law
And 3 at home with God
And those are just some of them.
My family is spread all across the world.
From a grandma who is Irish, to cousins in the Philippines,
And one little cousin who is both.
My family has every type of person you can imagine.
From the army to computer managers
to teachers to pastors
and then to the marines.
My family is a group of people
who I know got my back when the going gets tough.
And my family is one thing I know I will hold on to forever
until I may join them
with God.

Year
by Grace Weaver

A Year is 365 days.
A Year is 52 weeks.
A Year is 8,765.812 hours.
A Year is happy.
A Year is sad.
A Year has nights.
A Year has days.
A Year means life.
A Year means death.
A Year means milestones.
A Year means setbacks.
A Year means spring.
A Year means summer.
A Year means autumn.
A Year means winter.
A Year is aging.
A Year is time going by.
A Year feels like forever.

Dreams of You
by Russell Washington

I lay awake at night dreaming of you
How much you have changed, I dream about us being together again
I dream of your jokes and stunning laugh
I see you standing there waving me closer
but as I step forward the world slowly starts to crumble
Maybe I loved you too much
In each dream your sweet voice calls my name as you wisp away
into the darkness your face fades and the sky goes gray
I wake up sweating but done
the sweat turns to tears as I realize you're gone

New York City
by Kate Roche

The loud noises
Will only last a little longer
Until night takes over
Revealing the bright beautiful lights.
The sounds begin to slow down
This lovely city is composed of 5 parts:
Manhattan, Brooklyn, Bronx, Queens,
and Staten Island
Broadway, Empire State, Times Square,
and The Statue of Liberty
all in one spot.
The Big Apple
The City That Never Sleeps
The city so nice they named it twice
New York, New York
The city made for open-minded people.
The city full of opportunities and dreams,
Seems like the city for me.

Loss
by Marley Bongart

When you lose the most important person to you
you wish you can never relive the moment when it happened
like it never happened
you will always have that picture in your mind
the memories will never escape
everyone else will be hurt,
but not as much as you
nobody will ever feel as hurt as you
almost like the biggest thing in your life is gone
like your life is missing something

Depression
by Elexys McDowell

I'm sad. Not because I failed my last test
Or I forgot to do the dishes
But because I am depressed.
Do you see the smile on my face
Or my soul trying to escape
This unworthy fate
And please, don't get me started on religion
I believe in equality
Whether you're an immigrant, Muslim, or in prison.
Why is it always my fault?
When someone hates me, de-friends me
Never mind, I'll just go back in my little vault.
And don't worry. Despite my sadness
I'll never commit suicide
I love and hate my life so much
That I'm willing to go in mystified
I'll go on horrified
But most importantly
I won't give up because
I know I'm strong to keep doing what I thought was not enough

Ode To Ashley
by Devon Horn

The star of my very soul,
and eyes that sparkle like diamonds.
In the shadows we stay
laughing and dancing all the way
Your beauty never ceases
to amaze me.
Your voice sounds of pure silk,
that convinces me to do anything.
If you leave
I will always
carry you right beside
my heart
If I had the power
to control stars
I would make a constellation
of you

Day
by Connor Lang

Day
A day
One day
24 hours
1,440 minutes
86,400 seconds
Some days are fast
Others slow
But a day is a day
It is past
Present and future
A day leads to an eternity
A day can be bland and nothing happens
get up, go to work or school and go home but that one day
when something happens that you remember forever
Life starts
And ends
In one day
A day
Day

Roller Coaster
by Emily Nolen

The car stopped fast
My turn had finally come
I took a deep breath.
The car climbed up
Higher and higher I went
I soon went down fast.
The wind blew my face
I accelerated down
I feel very sick.

Happy Birthday ...
by Kiersten Busch

"Happy Birthday!" I would like to say,
But I can't, because I know you'd just push me away.
I can't believe it's been a year.
If you'd just rethink ...
But no. You hate me.
I get it.
Or do I?
When I see you,
I don't know if I want to hug you,
Or hide from you.
So I just keep my head down.
No use screwing it up more.
I would love to march over to you,
Hug you and say,
"Happy Birthday!"
But I can't.
You'd just scoff. And glare.
And tell me to leave you alone.
I think I understand.
Happy Birthday ...

Ode To Self-Worth
by Nikole Koenig

Feeling of self
Is everything we live for
To have
A place
A family
A body
That welcomes us with open arms
Saying we've missed you
That you are worthy to be here
In the crazy world just because you are you
Self-worth has been discontinued in our generation
Yet we crave it

The Dreams
by Nina Willis

Every night, I crawl into a hole and dream.
I dream of great pine trees and a river
where by its edge, the flowers grow.
On the horizon,
the mountain covers the pure silver moon
and geese fly back home to their nests
while the wolves triumphantly cry to the east.
I dream of a hall of kings
with feasting aplenty and scarlet banners
where everyone can be jolly.
They share stories of victory and happiness
while exchanging words of wisdom and joy.
I dreamt one night that I was an eagle.
I soared over the great big forest
only to perch upon your shoulder.
Bright yellow eyes staring into dark ones
and soft white plumage being touched softly
by your frail, pale fingers.

Ode To Mike
by Jennifer Gau

Oh my dearest Michael,
you drive me crazy.
You have me running in circles
like a cat chasing yarn.
It would be easier to catch the train.
Even though you're 12 years older than me,
your teasing is unbearable,
like getting a shot at the doctor's office.
It would be easier to read a Bible,
no matter how long.
I hate you, I love you, both the same.
Even though with you teasing me, like a dog being teased with a treat.
You push me forward,
when I'm stuck in a rut.
You push me through,
no matter what.

The Remembered and the Affable
by Erica Kent

When I first entered His heart,
I saw people
Who exist purely in our
Hearts and flowers.
But when I see her,
I can't help but see only her.
The nostalgia gone,
The present and future in focus.
But what will become of
The gone?
I love that she will talk to me …
There's no confusion involved.
But the gone are so perplexing,
Why do I even try?
Yes, why DO we try?
Why do we try to peek into
Something so spiritual?
It's so blatant, I believe,
That we must protect their memories,
In the same way they guarded our hearts.

Untitled
by Daijah Patton

A place where I can speak without the bastard echo that "needs" to demean me
A society where everyone realizes that social media isn't where
anyone should post things that anyone can see,
that anyone can repost or snapshot on their screen
An economy where unpaid wages for the women go straight to the men races
A generation where I'm not counting the seconds over my ten fingers
of how much time it will take to change
Children of my age, do not deserve the pain they've been giving
in vain of their upbringing
I feel the world isn't the same, that the American dream
has become lyrics to a song and some kind of game
and the folks born in my decade will stop drowning
in the dumbfounded stupidity rather than turning it into
the educational knowledge we learn in school
Where their actions are wiser and they quit judging others
And maybe where someone will remember me as the girl
who wanted humanity back to peace

My Beauty
by Anaya Manley

I'm that light skin girl that has an average height.
But instead, everyone has the nerve to ask: "Why you look so white?"
I mean, am I actually that light that people really have to ask?
Well, how about this. Why don't I just wear a mask?
That way people will stop asking. They'll want to know the real me.
Find out my true colors might even feel me; try to kill me
Because I don't even have the energy to answer your silly questions
about me and my complexions.
They don't understand the pain that hits me.
And there is barely nothing that can even fix me.
Last time I checked I'M BLACK! And Black is beautiful no matter what they say
And I know if I told them that they'd try to make me feel some type of way.
But that's just who I am and I'm not afraid to show it
I consider myself gorgeous, and I know it.
I may not be perfect or accepted the way I want to,
But I'm a QUEEN full of beauty, believe me if you want to.

Life In This World
by Lauren Czymek

We all live in the world,
We try to be one.
We live in the world,
But the war has begun.
We all play in this world,
Happy and healthy.
We play in this world,
But some people are stealthy.
We all fight in the world,
Trying to work together.
We fight in the world,
It seems to last forever.
We all leave the world,
Our family surrounding us with love.
We leave the world,
Some love ones waiting for us from above.

Life
by MaCall Smith

You feel completely and utterly alone.
Like you're dealing with life all on your own.
It's okay to cry, it's okay to hurt,
Because you're tired of being treated like dirt.
When you're wondering how you'll get through the night.
Feeling that there's no hope in sight.
Hold on. Push through.
You have no idea what life has in store for you.
You're unique, and wonderful in your own way.
All you have to do is make it through one more day.
Life has a way of working itself out.
Even when your head is filled with self doubt.
It's a lot easier said than done.
But there's nothing you can't overcome.
One more sunrise, one more day.
There's nothing that can stand in your way.
Right now you're wondering how?
But someday you'll look back and say look where I am now

It's America
by Danielle Arters

The sun shining down on the place we love,
Making the Red, White, and Blue shine out ever so brightly,
As the flag stands, it tells a story,
A story about freedom and acceptance,
A story about heroes that saved our home,
It's the stories and heroes that we will remember,
For eternity they will last,
The stories sweep over every state like a broom,
Picking up every detail and pushing it towards the symbol of freedom,
It's America.

Touch
by Olivia Korman

Nothing can one touch,
Without being touched by it.
Touch elicits touch back.
Touch, at first physical, then,
Transforms into emotions touched, moved by texture.
Softness makes a bond,
Creates a sense of belonging.
While roughness of the grass,
With fear of public stages,
Touches a nervous stomach, sending forth butterflies.
Sharp grief touches the soul,
The cut, leading to the seeking of connection to love.
The engraved face speaks to the inside,
Touching one self, causing the self to emerge.
Touch, the power of all senses,
Overcomes seeing, hearing, tasting,
And smelling.
Touch possess passion,
Passageways to unlocking
The soul.

All About Life
by Aiesha Pilant

When you are a baby, you are cuddled with joy.
When you are a child, you can play with your toys.
When you're a teenager, you are desperate for love.
When you move from your house, you are cold without gloves.
When you go get married, you go and say, "I do."
When a family flares, that just gave you the clue.
Your life is half-way done, your kids are in college.
Now you are retired, and have lots of knowledge.
Soon, you and your husband, get Alzheimer's disease.
you cannot remember macaroni and cheese.
When you are at the end, and your kids say goodbye.
you can't remember them, but closed your eyes and died.
Be positive a lot, and love the life that's charred.
When life just knocks you down, get back up and fight hard!

The Long Lost Treasure
by Matthew Witterholt

Looking. Searching. Finding.
Water, swaying back and forth
Salty sea air, whistling in my ears
Looking for what is needed
The long lost treasure
Looking. Searching. Finding.
Seagulls, squawking constantly like an alarm clock
Cousins, searching for tiny tan crabs
Searching for truth
The long lost treasure
Looking. Searching. Finding.
Seaweed, as green as newly cut grass
Fish, multicolored and going wherever the water takes them
Finding the wanted prize
The long lost treasure
Looking. Searching. Finding.
Satisfaction when the prize is found
The goal, finally met
The long lost treasure
Looking. Searching. Finding.

My Thoughts
by Erisa Pikuli

24/7 you're constantly on my mind,
you run around for hours and never get tired,
Those eyes of yours that I admire,
Everyone else is so oblivious and blind.
You make me feel a certain way,
My stomach has butterflies when I see you come around,
Whatever you want I'm down,
I'll go with anything you say.
You're the only one I want and the only one I need,
The way that your gaze haunts makes me wonder what I can mean to you,
Yet I feel invisible.
You're the thunder to my lightning,
you're my everything,
until I found out we had nothing.

Life. House. Fire
by Jessica Wagner

The Whites are the matches
The Blacks are the houses
The Grays are the smoke
It all started before we woke
The Whites start the fire
The Blacks burn
The Grays get caught in between
When will we learn?
The labels lead nowhere
Somehow we don't care
But when it turns on us
It's a big fuss
We riot for it to stop
But it starts with us to make it flop
In the end we will all be the match
That starts the fire and ignites the light

Unique
by Tajanna Mosley

You are unique in your own way.
No one is the same.
Don't let people bring you down.
And treat you like a clown.
Jealousy is everywhere.
But you should never care.
God made you for you.
So cherish your beauty too.
You are unique in your own way.
Say that every day, OKAY!

Skyrim
by Leila El Manfaa

Along the horizon shrouded by light
The slow setting sun shall give way to night
I stand beneath the black satin skies
Stars like twinkling crystalline eyes
Off in the distance, a lonely howl
And out come the wolves as they snarl and growl
Soon, their sounds fade away in the breeze
that swept through the leaves on the tops of the trees.
Silence returns like the black of the night
The stars by now risen to staggering heights
But there's something else that looms just as high
Something with wings as black as the sky
A formidable mass in the light of the moon
With its ear-piercing screech, its signature tune
And from its jaws came a pillar of blaze
And when the flame faded, only ashes remained.
But what is this fantasy world I've described?
A place with blue waters and dragon-swarmed skies?
A world one could only see in a dream,
Behold, the magical land of Skyrim.

A Rude Awakening
by Monica Skinner

Daylight grows as night shrinks away,
locked behind closed doors
Trapped in my brain, don't know what to say,
my heart pounds as it roars
I awake to the sounds of an explosive cry
it sent chills down to my spine
My chestnut eyes opened wide
I prayed that everything was fine
The ghostly whistle whispered to me
I hurried and ran to dress
Deep dark shadows where I could not see
my short breaths caused by distress
I softly crept down the stairs
blinded by tears from fear
I bumped into several chairs
the whistling was louder to hear
I peeked in the room and I could see
My dad was just boiling water for tea!

Ballad of a Brown Girl
by Kashaf Zaman

Some of us are canvases painted black
and we absorb the beauty of the world.
Some of us are canvases painted white
and we reflect that beauty.
Some of our canvases are a mix of different colors
and we do a little of both.
But we're all still God's masterpieces.
That's at least what I tell myself.
And I'm ...
BROWN.
The color
of the earth
of sturdy wood
of sun-sweet soil
and warmth.
They call me an "ABCD"
"American-born confused Desi"
But labels can't change my direction, 'cause I already know where I'm going.

Spring
by Sami Perkins

Colors fast
Like a cat onto a mouse
Fresh cut grass
A sticky sweet scent today
Flowers dance
Swaying to their own rhythm
Summer stance
Bursting at confound stretched seams
New fauna
Breath a crucial part of life
Mild sauna
Extreme weather soon to come

Warrior
by Kaira Poland

I am a lone warrior fighting my own battles,
While being the light of the darkness arise.
And being the dark horse that always wins
different battles that come my way.
Adversaries slay me with their harsh words,
They left wounds
They healed and turned into scars
These scars reminded me that the words will hurt now,
But, I will grow from these experiences.
I have my sword to defend me from my opponent's actions,
I have my armor to protect my heart from being broken,
I have my helmet to shield my head from the harsh words and comments,
And I have my shield to shield from the negativity.
I watch what I say because my mouth is my weapon,
I don't let my pride and my ego make my soul as dark as coal,
Instead, I make sure what I said is as pure as gold.
Each day, I take on a different battle and I fight
I fight for what I want.
As I open these doors, the greatest battle that I am still fighting is
LIFE!!!

Questions Left Unanswered
by Hope Stollsteimer

Why am I so ugly?
Why are others so much prettier?
Why can't I be good at drawing?
How come I can't sing?
Why do I suck at sports?
Why am I so bad at life?
What do people really think of me?
Why can't one guy like me?
What is wrong with me?
Do my friends actually care about me?
If I died who would cry?
Would I go to Heaven or hell?
Why are my teeth so crooked?
Why can't my smile be nice?
Why do I laugh so much?
How come I'm awful at running?
Why can't I be stylish?
These are my
Questions
Left unanswered

Until Tomorrow
by Sydney Bules

The sun plunges into the horizon, drifting into a deep sleep,
leaving behind bright colors to efface the familiar blue sky.
Sitting on a rusty, emerald swing,
listening to the harmony of the metal chains in the subtle breeze,
a cherubic face smiles at the comeliness of the organic canvas.
The swing, a pillow with wings of a butterfly, lifts her high into the air,
above the clouds she travels, gripping the cold metal links tighter,
leaning back to see the world from a new perspective.
Despite any spasmodic jerks from the restrictive chain,
attempting to pull her back to reality,
her tranquility cannot be sullied, the swing set is her fortress.
Driving herself forward with the power of inertia,
releasing her grip, she lands among the mulch.
As she walks back inside, the feeling of pure calmness leaves her,
but only until tomorrow.

The Big Take Off
by Skylar Miller

It's the perfect day out. It's not too cool or too warm,
and the wind is blowing ever so slightly.
I see others laugh and go down the hill,
but I stand back and watch nervously.
My heart is pounding out of my chest,
my stomach twists and turns, I might throw up.
I can't believe that I'm actually going to do it.
I'm going to "fly" down the big hill.
My friends have done this so many times before,
but I'm a beginner, and I've never tried anything like it!
I look over at my friends and give them a nervous smile,
they smile back confidently and nod.
I know that now is my time to overcome my fears!
I hear someone counting, five, four, three, two.
I lie down, take a deep breath, and push.

We Are the World
by Aislinn Donahue

I am a person.
I am person who belongs to the world.
The world is my shelter,
A shelter that is falling through my hands.
The world can be a dangerous shelter.
I am not the only person who belongs to the world.
These other people cause this.
These people can tear you down and build you up.
I've learned that you can't trust everybody you meet,
Since they are not always the people you think they are.
There are good people and bad,
Loving and cruel,
Trustworthy and sneaky.
However, some people make a difference.
We can rise up against the bad,
We can stop the bullying,
Stop the wars and crimes.
Believe in yourself,
Don't let anyone get you down.
Do what you have faith in,
It could make a difference.
We are the World.

Catch and Release
by Madison Wynn

The dark, lonely and cold, she lived.
Once, she met a man who she wanted to be with.
She wasn't lonely nor cold for once.
For the man she loved was a bright butterfly in her dark, colorless life.
She caught him, as well as the feeling of love and joy.
Yet, there was a fear in her broken heart.
She knew she had to set him free.
Butterflies are not meant to be confined.
They both caught each other.
Although, she loved him more than he did her.
Yet, they set each other free.
It was a catch and release

Just Because
by Cassidy Dunn

Just because I'm happy
Doesn't mean I don't have a hard time with life
It doesn't mean my life is perfect
And it doesn't mean I get everything I want
Just because I'm nice
Doesn't mean I don't have feelings
Doesn't mean you don't hurt them
And it doesn't mean everyone is nice back
Just because I'm smart
Doesn't mean I know all the answers
Doesn't mean I have to be in every honors class
And it doesn't mean I'm not trying my best
Just because I'm me
Doesn't mean you can make fun of me
Doesn't mean you can push me aside
Doesn't mean you can ignore me
Sometimes I'm not always happy
I'm not always nice
I'm not always smart
But I am always me

Just Because
by Tayler Washington

Just because I'm mixed
Doesn't mean I'm more black than I am white
Doesn't mean I'm more white than I am black
And doesn't mean I prefer one race over the other
Just because I keep it classy
Doesn't mean I'm a priss
Doesn't mean I'm prude
And doesn't mean I think I'm better than you
Just because I'm nice
Doesn't mean I like you
Doesn't mean I'm a pushover
And doesn't mean you can treat me like a doormat
I am who I am
Ashamed? Not the slightest bit
People expect things from me based on what they hear and see,
not from what they know
Now tell me honestly, were you expecting this?

The Sidewalk
by Brandon McCoy

We walk the streets every day,
And yet there is something that we always used to do so
Most of us just take it for granted
Which is why we must respect it.
What is it you ask, would I know?
Of course, it is the pathway of our lives,
Leading us everywhere
It is the sidewalk.
The sidewalk is what takes us where we must go
It is our guard from the danger waiting in the road
Much more than a path of cement slabs,
It is our way through life.
Without it, we would have no guide in life,
No path to follow,
Nowhere to go,
And no protection from danger.
Next time you go for a walk,
You will use the sidewalk
And even if you don't notice that it's there,
It will always offer you a guiding hand.

Gifted
by Jen Brace

"What's the capital of Bangladesh?"
The third grader says to a 'gifted' peer, laughing.
They don't know what 'gifted' means.
Her classmates cheer when she is picked for their team, but only for review games.
They become friends with her so she'll help them with homework.
They don't know why she never smiles.
They think she has everything, good grades, straight 'A's.
They don't know why she's always missing school.
"Doesn't being 'gifted' mean you like to do homework?"
It means finishing the worksheet
in the time it takes your partner to sharpen their pencil.
It's the first thing anyone says about you.
It's how everyone defines you.
"She's smart."

Reality
by Lauren Watkins

In my dreams,
I am stronger.
In my nightmares,
I am weak.
In my dreams,
I am loved.
In my nightmares,
I am hated.
In dreams,
I am a success.
In my nightmares,
I am a failure.
In my dreams,
I have hope.
In my nightmares,
I have given up.
In my dreams,
It's nothing but fantasy.
All my nightmares,
Are reality.

A Girl With Dreams
by Yesenia Hernandez

An inspiring writer whose life was cut short.
Not allowed to go places because of her yellow star.
Nine months later only to find out things are gonna go downhill.
Even all through this she tried to live a normal childhood.

Franks knew they were going to be found sooner or later.
Rejected to surrender to the harsh Nazis.
Adapted to her secret annex like it was her own home.
Nazis had forever ruined Anne's life.
Knew she wasn't gonna become what she wanted to be.

Why?
by Faith Brown

Why is that we hide?
We hide our true personalities,
the love we have for others,
and even the things we are most passionate about.
Why are we so ashamed of ourselves?
why do we care so much about what others think?
Being yourself is the most amazing thing you could ever imagine to be.
Stop trying to be what society wants you to be.
Be creative, be silly, be whatever you want to be!
So I say why care?

Ebony Night
by Sara Xibos

The chill sweeps across my skin
My curiosity pushes me forward
When my mind tells me to stay back
Is it night again, once more?
Have they come back, to take me away?
Or will they finally allow me to stay
For all I hear is crickets
Do they surround me?
There is light in the distance
I think it's spreading
What is life, is now awakening
For now, is my slumber

Society
by Breanna Boutte

We seek to find just who we are inside
Forever looking to find where we fit
Having constant fear of being denied
In the process some people just lose it
Everywhere we attempt to interact
Listening to them but not the words said
Little do we know it's all a fake act
None of us really knowing what lies ahead
We don't have to conform to the world's ways
We can be our self, stand up for belief
If we have faith and stay away from clichés
We will finally realize the relief
Pressure causing social anxiety
We stand here wrapped up in society.

Déjà Vu
by Jenna Suchower

If you know it's cold
don't go outside.
Someone else will.
Their lips may turn blue,
their skin may turn white,
and they might get lost in the snow.
But I think it's important to know
they will come back
and will be warmed right back up
by friends
by family
but not you.
You stand there looking on
thinking it should have been you
who went outside.

3rd Place

Amanda McNamara

Daydream
by Amanda McNamara

The tide tirelessly kisses her feet.
Her arm unfurls and dangles,
With no goal to meet.
Powdery velvet sand
Caresses the fingertips
Of her elegant hand.
Butterflies of an extravagant blue
Flirt and flutter lazily by.
Angelic breezes rustle the knowing yew,
Whispering softly in her ear,
"You are freed from worry.
Your struggles are over. God is here."
It took eternity for her to understand
There is no need for anxiety.
God carries us in His hand.
Peace. Peace. Peace.

Morgan Dennis

Social Media
by Morgan Dennis

She has 531 followers whom she calls friends
She talks to them online– she's never actually met them
She claims she isn't lonely, but she's always looking down
Down upon the screen of a modern smartphone.
Sharing information to websites and apps,
All online for others to access.
She goes out to dinner with a group of friends
As they sit in silence on their phones, discussions end.
Are they having fun? Well I suppose.
I wouldn't know, their expressions are unknown.
She posted up a photo onto a social website
Faking a smile, hiding her actual state of mind
The photo reached 200 likes,
That is what matters at this time.
As she types "lol" she doesn't crack a smile
Texting is essential– it is part of her lifestyle
She lives in a world
Dependent on electronics
Social media is anything but social
Isn't that ironic?

1st Place

Kyle Macaluso

From this talented 9th grade student
comes some very intriguing work.
Kyle's use of imagery masterfully piques ones' curiosity
in a poem that begs to be read and reread.
Excellent!

Interlude
by Kyle Macaluso

Two weeks before,
I told him another story, he sipping his decaf mocha.
On occasion he'd chuckle,
thin lips smirked, blue eyes narrowed, their corners crinkled.
One week before,
steam rose from his mug, its path obstructed by his hanging head.
Once I finished my story, he stood and left,
leaving his drink untouched.
The day before,
he was uncombed and unshaven.
I started my story as he sat, and in exasperation he whipped his head up,
thin lips wavering, blue eyes gone bloodshot, dark circles underneath.
On the day,
his seat was empty.
The day after,
a woman filled his empty seat, she sighing after every gulp of her latte.
I asked if she would like to hear a story.

Division IV

Grades 10-12

Two Souls
by Lauren Bules

Time is selfish, paying humans little heed.
It does as it pleases, taunting us from the past
As we recall a lost cause, another broken deed.
And we can only hope he won't decide this day is our last.
Fate is Time's cousin, but it's the more terrible.
It has no respect for love, plans, or uplifting hope.
Fate has the power to turn a perfect life unbearable.
Its destruction can create trouble of unimaginable scope.
These two violent souls walk hand-in-hand.
If life is a beach, Fate is the sea and Time is the sand.

Everything That I've Dreamed
by Diane Pak

Will I lose you forever or will you be mine?
I'm scared to live in the lie, when I can't handle the truth.
I love you yearly and every day I woke up and realized
this isn't the life I'm supposed to be in, even there isn't you in my future.
I know that you should pick someone who will always put a smile on your face.
Everything of you is fragile to my heart
Every day I look forward to seeing you, even if it's just for a second.
To be lying next to you, seeing you for the first time.
To be wondering and wishing who can see the beauty in your eyes.
The common and the certain things are able to cherish the moments forever.
It weakens the soul to see you get upset or hurt.
To see you happy is one of my favorite pictures that outstands any other picture.
My soul is at circumstance where it's even a longer distance
and a bigger differences between us.
My bleeding heart aches to see what the future rely on.
My mind controls the heart beating of my chest saying
"I will always keep the love safe in my heart."
The beating of the heart is a one-in-a-million places to be happy.
Will you be happy with me when life turns around
and come at times to be funny, sad, happy or serious?
Will you promise me that no matter where I'll be, you'll be here?
– Dedicated to Prince Sébastien of Luxembourg

Until the Day
by Bailey Ray

They curl under and spiral like a tornado
down till the wave rides out,
My body is right in the middle
feeling pressurized all around.
It starts with hitting you in the face,
as if sticking your head out a window at 100 mph,
then to your hair,
pulling it by every root.
All the while, your body is lifted
as high as the wave's high,
then gently set back down.
Questions you didn't even think to ask,
they get answered.
Re-found spirit, motivation, and purpose,
the dark heart never existed.
Good with good intentions,
the feeling brings me back.

Made Up
by Daria Paxton

Looking around, nothing's significant
Nothing I need
Not even a little bit
Look some more
Found a book
Made up stories
Made up faces
Useless times and places
Just words
A front and a back
Read a few lines
Didn't stop
Couldn't stop
These made up stories
These made up faces
Were part of the world
They were something bigger

For My Dad
by Jaxcia Hess

As soft winds sweep away the days, I look back at life through a haze,
Remembering playgrounds and friends, in a childlike gaze that never ends.
The laughter in a game of catch, shall memory ever attach ...
To innocence in my youthful eyes, catching the ball to your surprise.
I recall my first bike, my first wreck,
Who picked me up and said, "What the heck?"
You convinced me to give one more try,
While knees skinned I forgot to cry.
There was nothing I couldn't do,
My heart held fast that to be true.
Though some years are kinda rough,
I'm sure not too big or not too tough.
You taught me to defend what's right,
To never back down from a fight.
So I learned how to stand,
Even though with every bump I will fall,
I will always find your hand.
Me, drawing from you an inner strength
and a kind of stubborn pride of equal length,
But there the line of fate was drawn,
It was as if I blinked and you were gone.

Girls Lives Matter
by Lely Le

They say this is a man's world, that a woman can't make it out here.
Say that we are to play with Barbie dolls and dress up
just to make up for the things we cannot do.
Well, girls lives matter too.
We are not one, we are a whole, we are the future that tomorrow brings,
we shouldn't be seen as ghosts from days past
for everything we do in this world will last.
We are allowed to get our hands dirty,
to fix pipes that pipe up the heads of these men
who think we can do nothing more than serve them on hand and foot
but no honey, girls lives matter too.
The toys of tomorrow won't be Barbie thc teacher or the doctor or nail polish
for girls far too young to even understand what the label says
we are not what the label says, we can be so much more than that.
Be proud to be a girl because
Girls lives matter too.

A Bloodied Hell
by Natalie Birdsall

I look around me
The bodies of the fallen lie upon the field, breathless, lifeless, dead.
They stare at me with glazed-over eyes, seeing my horrors
but still seeing nothing at all.
I fall to my knees in agony, and the bloodstained grass seeps beneath me.
I cry out with torment but no one hears, for no one has the ability.
I am the last soldier standing.

H
by Katie Fleck

I hope that when the world ends,
I live long enough to see cities fall.
Callused hands like braille
a book for those who lack sight
or know not the pain
endured by these hands.
They've run themselves over one
and one thousand things.
Both beautiful and
less than beautiful.
Ugly,
and less than.

Words
by Sami Perkins

Hopelessness, sorrow, fault, inadequate,
Happiness, fun
Turmoil, hatred, anger, unforgivable,
Love, laughter
All emotions raw under a microscope
Kept bottled up not at all like a TV soap
All can be challenged by a single word
The word that kills
Dreams, hopes, desires, unity,
The word for the better or worse
It can be any particular word
As long as it has meaning
To you

Rain
by Leah Lundquist

The dark clouds roll in
Ominously they wait there
Then the rain pours down
It drenches the sky and ground
Leaving the Earth fresh and clean

Body Shaming
by Adrianna MacKenzie

Your body is your home
inhabited by one, alone,
yet judged by the world
day and night,
flesh through bone.
Too tall, too fat,
too round, too flat.
Society grins, throwing stones
Ones who catch them will be weighed down
try to compensate, but will drown
Sinking, sinking, through the ground
into the sea of insecurities.

Secrets of a Locked Away Heart
by Zyonna Boykin

She lay lonesome on her ruby stone,
Entwined by the golden locks in which it calls home.
Her smile plain and clearly not real,
For her eyes tell how she truly feels.
Sadness overwhelms her beautiful brown eyes,
As they turn like the stone that lies with inside.
Her beauty seems as the day and days before;
Though within her, she is truly sour and sore.
She lay there in darkness, silent,
Not even did she give her story a start.
She had already begun to fall apart;
For that ruby stone in which she laid upon
Was her locked-away heart.

Beauty Is ...
by Chloe Arthaud

Beauty is
It's in,
the receding line of snow,
the blooming buds on each tree,
and the new petals on sprouting flowers.
It's felt,
on every golden ray of sun,
on each cool splash of water,
and on the days surrounded by broiling heat.
It's everywhere,
in each wind that whisks away the autumn leaves,
in the skeleton trees,
and in the morning frost that laces each and every blade of grass.
It glows,
within the falling snow,
within the early fall of the freezing night,
and within the ice that seals the ground beneath.
Beauty is.

Everlasting Chains
by Preston Roe

Chains don't live,
Chains don't die.
Chains only bind us,
Scorched under sky.
We all have our chains,
Yet, few of us escape.
Our chains simply hold us fast,
Binding our will,
To meet a fate worse than death,
Everlasting still.
Yet, every link we forged ourselves,
To hold us to this place,
Our fear, our sorrow, our worries
and every lack of grace.
They hold us like chains,
To the same forsaken spot.
Shrug off your chain,
The chain is forged of fear,
but we want to be contained.
Cowardice is all that keeps us here.

We Live, We Die
by Henry Uribe

We live in a dark world
One in which truths hide behind lights
We live in a dark world
One in which lies are there in plain sight
We live in a dark world
Where peace is just a thought
We live in a dark world
Where war is always fought
We live in a dark world
That values money much more than lives
We live in a dark world
That can only wait for death to arrive
We live in a dark world
And the only thing promised is death
We live in a dark world
And you must be grateful for every breath
We die in this dark world
And leave behind our book of life
We die in this dark world
And hope our pages help uncover the light

A Wish To the Mirror
by Jhade Gales

Mirror Mirror on the wall, won't you grant me just one wish at all?
It's not something too big, yet neither too small.
Just one wish is all I ask for, from the mirror on the wall.
It's not for revenge,
Nor is it for love,
What I wish is something better than all of that.
It may be materialistic, but do not fret.
What I wish for goes further than all of that.
Mirror Mirror on the wall, won't you grant my wish at all?
No shoes, nor clothes
I have people to get me those.
Not a cat or a dog
I can adopt one of those.
Neither brains nor brawn
I can work for most of that.
All I wish for from the mirror on the wall is ...
My own personal chef!
Mirror Mirror on the wall, grant me this, and I'll never ask again.
For nothing at all.

From Here To There (My Changing Vision)
by Nicholas Rasmussen

Here I am is where I think I am today.
But where I am can be hard to really say.
Where I am depends on where I want to be.
Where I want depends on what it is I see.
Moving on from here along the way to there,
Old things move aside and new things do appear.
If something new is where I would rather be,
Then where I am becomes something new to me.
Only moving forward allows me to know
Where I really am and where I really go.
Only moving forward allows me to see
Who I really am and who is really me.
Who I am is who I think I am today.
But who I am can be hard to really say.
Who I am depends on who I want to be.
Who I want depends on who it is I see.

Rain
by Justice Dalton

I hear rain
It sounds like a new beginning
Sounds like a silly little thing
But it's not
I feel rain on
My skin
I feel the past
Get washed away, away
I see how it cleanses
The Earth with its beauty
Like fire, fire
I feel my soul set the
Storm free, free
Rain changes everything, everything
A new beginning, a past getting
Flooded out by a raging river,
Cleaning and repairing
Rain is a sacred thing
That can't be tampered with, with

Perfectly Imperfect Love
by Rania Abdel-Moomen

From the first day I laid my eyes on you,
I already knew we were meant to be.
Right away we fit together like glue,
Even though at times we may not agree.
Sometimes I might slap you and curse at you.
Then get mad and not want to talk to you either,
But through it all I know our love is true.
I'm never letting go of you either.
It makes me feel blessed being by your side.
You're very special to me and not like the rest.
I can't wait until I become your bride.
My darling, you are just the very best.
Me and you created the perfect crime.
We stole each other's hearts from the first time.

Hands
by Cara Ludovico

In February, we first locked eyes from across the room,
I could see the green sparkle as your feverish smile tempted for more.
All I wanted was to hold your hand.
By April, we had been on two dates,
You held my hand as we danced in the rain.
We went home drenched in the idea of each other.
In June, I was madly in love.
Each time we kissed,
I felt as if I were way past cloud nine and in a whole new world.
In August you told me how sad you were
and how the stress was getting to be too much.
At the end of the night we held hands and I fell asleep
to the sound of your convulsing chest.
By October, you were gone.
The sadness had become too much
and the darkness from within had swallowed you whole.
When December finally came, the burning of your skin was no longer to be felt.
I finally threw away your stuff and you were buried six feet under
along with my love for the feel of your
Hands.

A Flower Named Sakina
by Alleh Naqvi

A flower once danced in the Sun's rays.
The innocence of her heart shining through her name.
She was a forgotten flower lost in time.
As I realize it was her, the daughter of Light.
I hear her weeps in my sleep, see the tears run down her cheek,
And I cannot seem to relate to her pain.
She sees the burning tents ablaze with red and bodies lay dead.
She hears the cry as the sword strikes her Light.
I see her through my eyes and wish I was there by her side,
And learn a lesson about a real fight.
The flower was left to weep blood tears, and I left to lament.
That day that marked the rise of darkness never ends.
Evil embraced as her light was killed.
The flower wilted and now she sleeps with the dead,
Forever trapped in the dark.

I'm Done
by Michael Katchuk

I'm done
I'm tired of all of your nonsense
I'm tired of putting, waiting around, waiting for you
I'm not gonna do no more, I'm done
Finished.
Once I say I'm done, I'm done for good
There will be no turning back
You said you love me and care about me
That was a lie, wasn't it
I'm tired of just waiting for you
Because you say all this stuff, oh I love you
But did you really mean it though
I'm done with you and your nonsense
I'm not going to stand here waiting no more
I'm moving on
I don't need you checking up on me anymore
I don't need you pretending to care
Most of all I went fifteen years without you
and I'll go the next fifteen years without you
But in the end you turned on me
I can't believe I waste my time on you
I can't believe what I put on the line for you
And it ends, I'm just finished with you

Turn Away
by Kassandra Ayllon

Exhausted from last night
Life not lost
Today we turn away
further from your jump,
parallel from pain

Words Unspoken
by Lauren Knecht

I knew of this.
Divided in two, our world
remains one side flowers
and the other embers.
While the embers may fade,
and new life may bloom,
the flowers on the first
will turn to dust soon,
and I regret to say
I knew of this.

She Has a Way
by Andrew Bridgewater

She has a way.
A way that my mind will never fathom.
She can create a smile on my face without trying.
She is beautiful in every way.
Her hair may not be the softest
Nor is her waist a zero, but still there are zero defects about her.
She isn't perfect, however, she is perfect for me.
Her beauty illuminates in the darkness.
Her voice creates a smile of brightness.
It's all too beautiful. She is beautiful.
So beautiful that a black hole couldn't swallow the light
And memories of love and laughter
She is truly a "once in a lifetime girl."
She is my "once in a lifetime girl."
And I love her to the end of the universe.
And even after that.

Naïve Greed
by Emily Moyer

We ravage and we rage
we burn and we haze
we torment and we corrupt,
all for a rock.
It's a magnificent rock,
with shimmering oceans in deep canyons
and budding vegetation bursting forward.
But a rock is a rock.
Our universe is expanding–
a child lost in eternal growth spurts,
and our precious Earth
is but a pebble in its grasp.
Yet people continue sinking into the sandpit of sin
with their children dipping their hands into that dreadful sand after them,
neither ever realizing the true prize is a gem
that we can never touch.

The First Body I Almost Drank
by Lauren Weiss

I was born yesterday
From the brine tracing
Roots on your body.
You lay there,
Adam,
A shimmer evaporating
From the sand.
I am thirsty.
I'll not be
Your acre,
A stretching plain soaked with sweet rain.
Don't get up–
Listen. My dress touches
The floor, spreads
Like a spill.
And I am thirsty.
I will take your fingers in my mouth
And consume
You.

Mask
by Sonia Castro

Halloween, parties, dances.
Those are the places where we are used to seeing them.
We don't realize that we see and wear them every day.
And because a smile isn't so obvious as to come with strings hanging off of it,
We never know how great of a mask it truly is.
People complain when others use make up
to cover up how they truly look and feel,
But they couldn't care less when those same people use a smile as a substitute.
In reality, we are like clowns,
We can have tears falling down our face,
But because there is a smile drawn on that's too life like to look fake,
we make fools of ourselves and believe each other when we say we're okay.
We have so many reasons to keep on a mask:
It's the most accessible mask there is.
It doesn't bring questions because it's so natural.
It can fool anyone,
Even those who consider themselves masters
of knowing when they're being deceived.
But, if we were to ask ourselves what's a good reason to take off this mask,
We would all find ourselves going silent.

The Color of Hope
by David Collie

A far off mountain, seemingly impossible to scale
upon reaching the summit, the view we behold makes us wish it was
fantastic tales of wonder and beauty waiting to be found on the other side
crushing reality of a desolate land, nearly devoid of the color promised
a disheartening sight, causing us to yearn for the beauty we left behind
we resign to begin our defeated return
seconds from retreat, we see an isolated wonder in the hopelessness ahead
a chromatic field of flowers amongst the overwhelming despair
such a delicate and fragile thing, yet amidst the tranquility
there were burning fiery reds, ferocious oranges, and zealous yellows
we remember the fields of childhood fondly
but the spectacle ahead was far more enticing than any display behind
the hopeful land sparks not only the will to climb down, but the desire
we see the darkness we'll be met with
but we continue on
even when discouraged by the surrounding graveyard of color
we know the fields of our past, will no longer satisfy.

Astronomical
by Jani Berghuis

love the astronomer and he
will show you the stars
in the sky
and an infinity of
faceless questions
but love the writer
and I
will find the stardust
in your freckles
and the answers
in your eyes

Dreaming of More
by Sierra Self

All my life, I have been child of the flame.
I swept my gaze across my demons and they trembled,
I trailed my fingers around their thoughts and they fled.
Only in my dreams did I truly get to experience the intoxicating fear
that left me hopeless and breathless all at once.
One night, in the depths of my slumbering mind,
I found myself racing across a still and barren wasteland.
Beyond my shrouded gaze tiny fractures in the skies
cried in silence for another world lost.
Scattered across the sands, rows of shattered stars reached for the heavens,
longing for the touch of darkness embracing them once again.
My feet pounded across the horizon
but not once did I flinch when the mourning stars pierced my flesh,
leaving behind a trail of forgotten blood.
The wind began to dance to the beat of my pounding heart
and from underneath my red footprints sprang convulsing hands,
unable to contain their desperate hunger for my visions of the past.
They reached for the illusion of freedom,
soul mirroring the selfishness they saw within me,
but all they could promise her was a life of grey, so she fled,
leaving behind only rusted chains.
There was no sound, only the thunder racing underneath my feet
and the lightning casting shadows that cared not of our boundaries
between sky and Earth, Heaven and Hell, imagination and reality.
In the end, they were all in the same.
Through the raging storm I left behind and the cold emptiness before me
longing for the sweet taste of disaster,
I could only wonder at the beautiful beast I must have been running from.

Forgetting Love
by Amber Verville

In nature's sweet embrace I lay,
To remember you one last day.
High above, sheep dance with whales.
Clouds all spinning different tales.
In the lonesome, beautiful space
I try to imagine your face.
Whilst jays and robins sing love songs,
They tell how I've felt all along.
Who were you to push me away?
What lie did my face say?
And in the quiet of ancient trees,
I try to forget my tearful dreams.
The woods so quiet, just birdsong.
What I needed all along.
To forget, to put away.
To store tears for another day.

Tamed Lips
by Angelina Cortes

With tamed lips
She whispered his name
Though, in the silence, her dark cloud grew
With the taste of sugar
On her tongue
And the sweet melody
Of a blue bird's song, that is what beauty was
But with quivering lips
She yelled his name
Though, in the silence, there was no reply
And the appearance of others could not sway her
And his smile could not make her cry
For she did not have eyes to see
And her dark cloud was very large
But with tamped lips
She whispered his name.

America
by Caleb Thuernagle

I am equal
I am free
I am peaceful
I am spree
I am majestic
I am opportunity
I am epic
I am unity
I am friendly
I am just
I am ready
I am robust

Fireworks
by Camille Kurtz

I have never fought in battle
this I know to be true
And yet I like to think I've seen it
within the skies of blackish blue
'Twas no question that the dominance
of which each side bestowed
Echoed forth in greens and oranges and reds
as such as seen in the metals that corrode
Bright was the firing of the shots
and oh so loud the shouts
I swear it sent me looking back and forth (and up and down)
and people running roundabout
The crash and clamor as each side collided
the impact of the foes with ethereal might
I never stopped to question how
Each maintained in such a fight
Of the casualties I'm afraid to say I know none
and the victor, too, I cannot declare
For how should I know who hath won
the clash of such a pair?

3rd Place

Paulina Camara

Tellurian Innocence
by Paulina Camara

In the blistering days of her youth
Her father would tower over her
Providing her shade while she leaned on him
He would whisper very quietly
Of how she was born for this world
And how this world was born for her
The soft dirt would meet her small feet
As she ran to pluck flowers that called her name
The sun would kiss her delicate shoulders
While the leaves simpered at the brief graze of her skin
When the wind would pick up, her father would dance with her
And her twirling would remind the moon of its celestial duties
She held the Milky Way in her lungs
And the stars in her eyes
And every day as the sun bid farewell
Long, dark outstretched arms awaited her
And she would run and hug her father close
The rough bark scratching her cheek lightly
As sunshine dripped from her hair
And nebulas spilled from her fingertips

Jodi Aleshire

To Be a Woman
by Jodi Aleshire

I am not yours.
My body is not your playground, your temple at which to worship
Keep your smudged fingers off, get your dirtied hands away
My story is not yours to alter, to twist, to rewrite for you alone
Do not tell me I am your Juliet, your Ophelia, Lolita, Rosalyn, Guinevere
I am not here for your eyes.
How do you have the gall to water me down all for your own consumption
I am broken glass sliding down your throat,
I am vinegar poisoning your wine
Do not try and soften my edges, smooth my cracks and ridges
Though bent, broken, bloodied, bruised, you tell me I must stay beautiful
I am a woman.
How dare you presume I am soft as silk, smooth as satin
They may tell you I am made of man, from his breath, his bones, his dirt
But honey, that was long ago, now men are made from me
Laced with thorns, but I am not a flower, touch me and I will make you bleed
I am not fragile.
Do not think I am just your sister, your mother, your daughter, your aunt
I will not burn my flesh to provide for you before myself
Hand me the tinder and I will laugh and leave it in my place as I leave
I am not yours to burn and I never was.

Madison Seabrook

When it comes to writing,
this high school senior has impressive credentials,
including three scholastic art and writing awards,
two silver medals and a best in grade poetry selection.
She has even published a book of one act plays and essays.
Following her dreams,
Madison plans to complete a college double major
in musical theater and cultural studies.
We wish her much success
and congratulate her on another fine accomplishment ...
this year's Editor's Choice Award.

Editor's Choice Award

Industria and Acedia
by Madison Seabrook

Diligence flicks her callused finger towards Sloth,
who slumps amongst a puff of dandelions tickling the edges of a pond,
his fingers taut with lymph that has settled around bones
the same way clouds seem to bloat over a sharp fragment of moon.
She tickles, under his chin, stubble like stingers caught in skin,
yet slick with the oils of a thousand naps.
She dreams they would run and dig for mussels,
laughing as children at those who sermonize
that only one can exist within each body.
Diligence's yellow fox eyes might only rest
after an eaglet has taken the first bit of air between his feathers.
Sloth's red clay eyes might only sharpen when she is near.
Sloth in a kaleidoscope does not split into colors,
but slides to the bottom of the tube.
Diligence flickers between the honeycomb prism,
tempting Sloth to come and play.
He who spends his time dreaming that he could invoke her into himself.
She who wishes she could lay her head on his steady chest.

Index of Authors

A

Abdalla, Sarah 104
Abdel-Moomen, R. 206
Acharya, Vir 49
Adams, Brenner 154
Agriss, RJ 130
Albert, Keira 33
Aleshire, Jodi 215
Altobelli, Andrea 72
Alvarado, Colby 88
Amorando, Olivia 104
Anderson, Bree 35
Anglesey, Trinity 144
Arcara, Brendon 112
Arnold, Allison 53
Arters, Danielle 179
Arthaud, Chloe 203
Ashcraft, Casey 29
Atkinson, Julia 69
Ayllon, Kassandra 208

B

Bagley, Aaron 17
Barclay, Connor 108
Barzousky, Lily 25
Bauer, Caden 122
Baxter, Kaelah 118
Bayer, Marlon 79
Beasley, Ashley 142

Beltran-Grémaud, Sibylle 47
Benson, Bridget 89
Beougher, Corey 17
Berghuis, Jani 211
Bergkoetter, Dean 45
Bernet-Aponte, Jonathon 132
Berrier, Emma Rose 160
Berry, Gage 18
Bewley, Tessa 88
Bianco, Niko 106
Bioteau, Gabrielle 162
Birdsall, Natalie 201
Bissey, Sami 38
Bjornlie, Dylan 69
Black, Matthew 16
Blanco, Chantel 67
Blick, Lauren 91
Bolden, Jennah 44
Bongart, Marley 172
Booqua, Tianna 4
Borda, Alexander 103
Boutte, Breanna 191
Boutte, Samantha 113
Boyd, Fisher 139
Boykin, Zyonna 202
Brace, Jen 189
Brady, Megan 133
Brasch, Braden 117
Breinholt, Joya 59
Bridgewater, Andrew 208

Bromgard, Layth 55
Brooks, Sierra 75
Brown, Faith 190
Brown, Sydnee 43
Bules, Lauren 198
Bules, Sydney 185
Burns, Ryan 151
Burrows, Dylan 124
Burz, Cristina 55
Busch, Kiersten 174
Byerly, Paige 111

C

Cake, Samantha 57
Calder, Aubrie 113
Camacho, Alondra 168
Camara, Paulina 214
Capella, Jeremy 155
Caraway, Kaleb 56
Carvalho, Amy 124
Castaldi, Joseph 78
Castillo, Alivia 41
Castro, Sonia 210
Catalano, Natalie 64
Cavallaro, Richard 81
Cerruti, Thomas 14
Chase, Brooke 166
Chavez, Darlina 163
Chhun, Lilly 73

Index of Authors

Chiem, Meady 23
Christensen, Wyatt 30
Chronowski, April 107
Chung, Trudy 79
Church, Sierra 51
Cianci, Stephen 93
Clark, Darian 147
Clark, Ella 30
Collie, David 210
Corridoni, Vincent 82
Cortes, Angelina 212
Cram, Amber 29
Cram, Seth 160
Crandall, Lindsey 43
Crespo, Matias 66
Czymek, Lauren 178

D

Dadourian, Brendan 31
D'Agostino, Kayla 166
Dalton, Justice 205
Davis, Cameron 28
Dennis, Morgan 193
DeTreux, Alexandra 87
DeTreux, Jacob 158
DiBricida, Luke 26
Dillard, Yaamir 162
Dirickson, Macie 16
DiVincezo, Aaron 130
Docimo-Ziccardi, A. 115
Donahue, Aislinn 186
Donapel, Maura Rae 79
Donohue, Asher 54
Dougherty, Emily 25
Douglass, Maizee 65
DuBeck, Matthew 126
Dumagco, Matthew 118
Dunham, Ethan 28
Dunn, Cassidy 187
Durtschi, Sera 17

E

Eddy, Erin 35
Eich Woodward, Z. 169
Eill, Samantha 115
El Manfaa, Leila 182
Everett, Nevaeh 10

F

Fagan, Erin 73
Fagley, Christopher 84
Fall, Benjamin 27
Fall, Ciara 19
Fam, Nadya 85
Feeney, Laura 121
Ferguson, Caitlyn 75
Fields, Adrianna 94
Flannery, Keely 21
Fleck, Katie 201
Flores, Cristian 168
Forbes, Amiera 45
Forbes, Justin 97
Ford, Charlie 108
Forehand, Amber 92
Foxhill, Olivia 87
Fredericksen, Logan 19
Frisch, Justen 135
Fu, Allison 125
Furtaw, Charley 80
Futrick, Carly 37

G

Gabelberger, Sophia 110
Galante, Isabella 149
Gales, Jhade 204
Garcia, Fiorella 47
Garcia, Kevin 16
Gardner, Allison 12
Garozzo, Ileona 68
Gaspar, Edgar 167
Gau, Jennifer 176
Glenn, Damian 106
Gonzales, Isabelle 21

Gonzales, Rhianna 119
Grable, Kelly 43
Green, Alexander 114
Greenwell, Paige 30
Grover, Dayton 52
Gudas, Emily 129
Guerricabeitia, Kepa 76
Guevara, Natasha 156
Gunter, Paige 154
Guruprasad, S. 127

H

Hadley, Alaina 13
Hadzick, Livi 132
Hafer, Kate 89
Hagen, Lauren 109
Haj, Yahmin 121
Hall, Calista 108
Hammond, Tia 146
Hancock, Mekenzie 90
Hands, Anthony 144
Hansell, Amanda 161
Harrington, Sean C. 13
Harris, Daysia 143
Hartbauer, Annamay 164
Haupt, Graham 69
Hellyer, Elloise 34
Helzner, Ben 153
Henwood, Allison 96
Hernandez, Yesenia 190
Hess, Baylee 159
Hess, Jaxcia 200
Hicks, Siera 164
Hill, Mekenzie 147
Hoene, Vanessa 31
Hoover, Morgan 70
Hope, Carly 82
Hopkins, Nicole 13
Horlacher, Isaiah 111
Horn, Devon 173
Hosendorf, Daja 161
Howell, Kennedy 100
Hubbs, Emmaline 105

Index of Authors

Hubmaster, Joey 93
Hughes, Jamal, Jr. 150
Hunter V, Oliver H. 157
Hutchinson, Rylee 99

I

Iannacone, Andrew 152
Iannacone, Megan 103
Ivashina, Alice 101

J

Jacobson, Calissa 167
Jarvis, Jaclyn 131
Jaskot, William 114
Jefferson-Philmore, D. 53
John, Isaac 134
Johnson, Jenna 98
Johnson, Tiernee 20
Joniec, Michaela 10

K

Kail, Emma 169
Kaplan, Daniel 134
Katchuk, Michael 207
Kaylor, Logan 42
Keck, Elijah 72
Kehs, Cassy 124
Kehs, Dani 117
Kelley, Kristin 145
Kendall, Ian 116
Kennedy, Bailey 65
Kennedy, Ian 87
Kenner, Quadree 92
Kent, Erica 176
Kirkmire, Chaney 63
Klahold, Dane 97
Klaiber, Caroline 76
Klempel, Amos 10
Klug, Sierra 125
Knecht, Lauren 208
Koenig, Nikole 175
Korman, Olivia 179

Kraines, Rosalie 49
Kramer, Cole 165
Kristoff, Daniel 91
Kurtz, Camille 213

L

Lai, Joshua 51
Lang, Connor 173
Lanzillo, Amanda 156
Lavigna, Sophia 38
Law, Alexis 46
Le, Kathleen 36
Le, Lely 200
Lelewski, Shawn 64
Lia, Lucas 120
Lind, Max 112
Lindsey, Korby 19
Lo, Ivy 75
Lopez, Kerry 51
Lu, Christina 50
Ludovico, Cara 206
Lundquist, Leah 202

M

Maar, Samantha 133
Macaluso, Kyle 195
MacKenzie, Adrianna 202
Madden, Mya 11
Makowicz, Noah 77
Malandra, Kate 39
Manley, Anaya 177
Marks, Aurora Grace 35
Marley, Jeneyan 92
Mason, Andrew 84
Mason, Taniyah 100
Massaro, Gabby 148
Massimiano, Ashlynn 82
Mayes, Payton 18
McCarthy, James 99
McCoy, Brandon 188
McCoy, D'Mar 33
McDonough, Emily 23
McDougall, Adessa 135

McDowell, Elexys 172
McFadden, Zahquesz 129
McKenna, Michael 81
McLaughlin, John 41
McLeod, Ricquela 83
McNamara, Amanda 192
Melfe, Giana 158
Mickens, Aaliyah 95
Miles, Nakiah 23
Miller, Elizabeth 107
Miller, Jade 40
Miller, Samuel 34
Miller, Skylar 186
Mitchell, Ashley 28
Moore, Clayton 36
Moore, Kassidy 153
Morena, Justin 67
Morrell, Levi 77
Morrow, Melina 123
Mosley, Tajanna 182
Moyer, Emily 209
Murray, Daniel 122
Myers-Poppay, Piper 90

N

Naqvi, Alleh 207
Nelson, Calai'f 94
Nelson, Peyton 85
Neuman, Ross 118
Newman, Andrew 110
Newnam, Izzy 152
Nguyen, Andy 160
Nolen, Emily 174
Nolt, Hannah 149
Nunez, Edgar 41
Nuxoll, Lilly 146

Index of Authors

O

O'Malley, Emily 154
O'Malley, Madison 44
Omundson, Xzander 46
Orapallo, Andrew 24
Orbin, Austin 156
Orsini, Nicholas 71

P

Pacheco, Luis 45
Pak, Diane 198
Palmer, Keiana 145
Paramo, Christian 122
Parkkila, Nastasha 89
Paski, Christina 83
Patton, Daijah 177
Paxton, Daria 199
Pearson, LoRon 40
Penkert, Hannah 66
Perez, Tony 12
Perez, Yamil 39
Perkins, Sami 184, 201
Perrigueur, Eleonore 54
Perrotta, Gillian 136
Peterson, Emily 68
Petrone, Sofia 48
Pettyjohn, Raymond 66
Pikuli, Erisa 181
Pilant, Aiesha 180
Plegaria, Jhoannie 128
Plourde, Brody 78
Poland, Kaira 184
Pospiech, Richie 157
Prosper, Tristan 52

Q

Quarles, Jay'Von 4

R

Rasmussen, Nicholas 205
Ray, Bailey 199
Rayburn, Ivy 52
Reliquet, Baptiste 55
Remacle, Allison 14
Remacle, Nicholas 11
Rex, Dylan 65
Richey, Felecia 155
Richmond, Jaleigh 11
Ricks, Kaleb 29
Roberts, Zoey 63
Roche, Kate 171
Roe, Preston 203
Rogers, Hannah 105
Rogers, Jannessa 95
Roy, Adrianna 99
Roy, Leah 143
Rozenbaum, Hannah 32
Ruggio, Sophia 168

S

Saint-Dic, Jaden 71
Sanabria, Nyla 86
Santos, Cynthia 70
Sauceda, Anjoelina 32
Sauerwald, Aubrey 116
Savage, Genevieve 39
Schied, Kalwin 64
Schlack, Chloe 101
Schmidt, Eve 123
Schmidt, Hannah 30
Schmidt, Liam 26
Schneider, Jessica 48
Schrag, Zachary 159
Scott, Jordan 96
Seabrook, Madison 6, 217
Sedeno, Sierra 31
Seklecki, Evan 44
Self, Sierra 211
Shallomita, Marciella 74
Shane, Kylie 74

Sharma, Sameer 107
Sharon, Ella 131
Shaw, Hannah 70
Shores, Tara 102
Shull, Alexa 71
Shumaker, Sydney 170
Silvestro, Sierra 157
Simmons, Parker 142
Skeels, Ryan 76
Skinner, Monica 183
Smack, Donald III 128
Smith, Karly 163
Smith, MaCall 178
Smith, Sage 135
Smith, Siani 72
Smith, Taniya 37
Smith, Tyliah 46
Snyder, Sophia 62
Sokolowski, Rachel 24
Sperry, Giana 71
Steffy, James 120
Stek, Devyn 27
Stollsteimer, Hope 185
Strunk, Ashley 32
Sturges, Adilyn 22
Suchower, Jenna 191
Swartz, Jacqueline 119

T

Talbot, Trecon 20
Taylor, Isabel 102
Thatcher, Kendra 151
The, Rio 86
Thiel, Emma 133
Thorn, Icheir 93
Thuernagle, Caleb 213
Tilley, Jaden 100
Tirtakusuma, Valkyrie 12
Tjandra, George 123
Toole, Angelina 155
Transtrum, Sam 106

Index of Authors

Trapani, Paola 22
Trimble, Jeffrey 15
Twery, Alex 126

U

Ujobai, Lindsay 25
Uribe, Henry 204

V

Valles, Laykin 22
Ventura-Soto, Leslie 134
Verville, Amber 212

W

Wagner, Jessica 181
Wagner Uhling, Elle 14
Wallacavage, Isabel 47
Ward, Hannah 91
Washington, Russell 171
Washington, Tayler 188
Watkins, Lauren 189
Wayenberg, Lexis 42
Weaver, Grace 170
Weber, Jade 62
Weiss, Lauren 209
Wenclewicz, Ryan 15
West, Kolby 98
Whipple, Martin Anders 109
Whitlock, Alexandra 21
Whitlock, Hailey 15
Wilkins, Dylan 148
Will, Daniel 117
Williams, Abby 68
Willis, Nina 175
Witterholt, Matthew 180
Wong, Sarah 50
Wright, Kathryn 127
Wynn, Madison 187

X

Xibos, Sara 190

Y

Yang, Alison 40
Yang, Elaine 137
Yu, Normen 150

Z

Zaman, Kashaf 183
Zelmanoff, Isabella 36
Zhang, Sarah 34
Zieba, Caroline 165
Zogar, Christina 95

Eloquence
Price List

Initial Copy 32.95

Additional Copies 25.00

Please Enclose $7 Shipping/Handling Each Order

Must specify book title and name of student author

Check or Money Order Payable to:

The America Library of Poetry
P.O. Box 978
Houlton, Maine 04730

Please Allow 4-8 Weeks For Delivery

THE AMERICA
LIBRARY OF POETRY

www.libraryofpoetry.com

Email: generalinquiries@libraryofpoetry.com

17